Restaurant Ridiculous

Slip and Fall Personal Injury Lawsuits

Negligent Acts

Management Fails

& Industry Solutions

Restaurant Expert Witness
Howard Cannon
©2025

Limitations and Considerations

Needless to say, it is impossible to put every relevant part of restaurant industry and OSHA standards regarding slip and falls in restaurants within this book and it is in no way intended to be a comprehensive or complete list of relevant knowledge.

This material is not intended to be legal advice. It is offered to the reader as is, with no warranties or guarantees that it is not with or without errors and/or omissions. We nor the publishers assume responsibility for liability or errors, omissions, loss, risk, and/or damages resulting from the use of, or reliance on, and/or application of this material.

In fact, this book has not been edited to professional standards because we very firmly believe that no one should wait until they are fully edited to come to Jesus any more than they should wait until they have all the answers to clean their restaurant floors.

So we do not assume any responsibility for any errors or editing needs you see within this book.

OSHA-specific material as well as other material we shared within this book is in the public domain and may be reproduced, wholly or partially, without permission of the Federal government and/or without authorization from OSHA or those other governing bodies. Other materials contained in this book are owned exclusively by the author.

Why We Use Crows

Crows are one of the smartest animals on the planet. So smart that scientists compare their brain to that of a 7-year-old human child. And just like your own little 7-year-old prodigy at home, they have absolutely incredible ingenuity, creative problem solving, and awareness of their surroundings. But instead of using it to throw a baseball through the window or get detention again at school, crows have used their minds to keep themselves safe and surviving in countless climates and regions of the world.

They have the common sense, they have the book smarts, they have a bigger vocabulary than a parrot, and can figure out how to get a piece of beef out of a Coke bottle with a wire clothes hanger. They are truly one of God's most impressive creatures.

They also have an amazing memory! So good that there's a family of crows who still hates my guts on the 6th hole of a Wisconsin golf course that I grew up next to. I bothered one of them as a teenager over 40 years ago and its entire family still hasn't forgiven me.

And in the restaurant business, you have to be aware just like those crows. You have to be smart. You have to be well-studied on the book smarts of industry standards while also using reasonable and basic common sense. You have to be hyper-aware of your surroundings, and you have to actually remember what you learn and experience. Otherwise, things can get ugly in the blink of an eye and someone's safety – or even their life – can be put in jeopardy.

If everyone were more like the crow, our restaurants would probably be a lot safer and I wouldn't have nearly as many cases come across my desk. So, like the crow, I hope you remember what you learn in this book to keep your customers safer or your clients better cared for.

That, my friends, is why we used our custom crow art inside this book – to remind you to be book smart and street smart for better safety for all.

It is my hope and prayer that this book serves you well for that purpose. Kindest regards and God's blessings.

The Three "R" Rules of Restaurant Training: Repetition, Repetition, Repetition

Spoiler alert: a major running theme in this book is training in restaurants and how the entire culture of a restaurant effects the safety of the joint.

And you'll find that the book talks about that – and a lot of other points – over and over and over.

That's because training is a function of *repetitiveness*. If you are going to train anyone in anything, you must repeat yourself more than what feels necessary. You can't just tell your kid how to throw a ball once, you have to instruct him or her over and over and get that kid to repeat that throw over and over and over again.

In a restaurant, you have to ensure that employees hear and repeat the operational instructions – like cleaning the floors properly – over and over and over again to cement it in.

It seems obvious, but too often we forget that we do not become what we are told or instructed. We become what we *practice* and *repeat*.

So just like the crows in the art pieces of this book who repeat behavior that works in order to survive, restaurants have to repeat the behavior that is up to industry standard to keep themselves and customers safe.

So, if you find that this book repeats itself a lot, get over it. It's part of your training. :)

Kindest regards and God's blessings again, and again, and again...

Contents

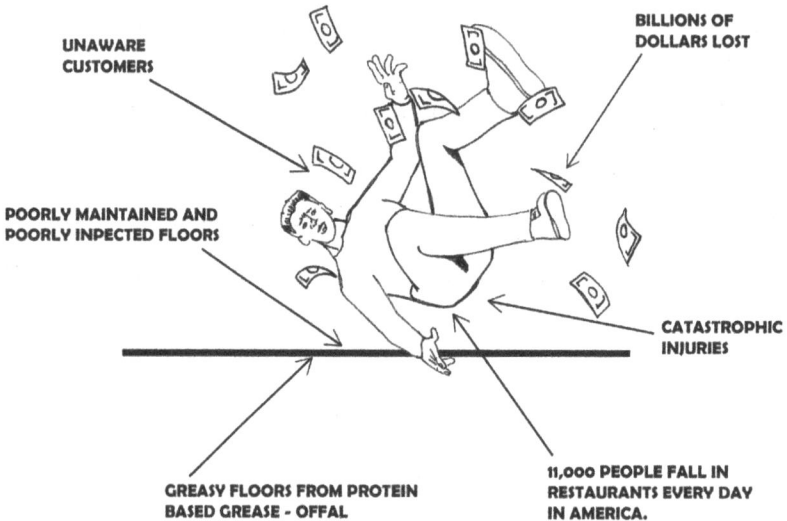

SLIP & FALLS ON GREASY RESTAURANT FLOORS

UNAWARE CUSTOMERS

BILLIONS OF DOLLARS LOST

POORLY MAINTAINED AND POORLY INPECTED FLOORS

CATASTROPHIC INJURIES

GREASY FLOORS FROM PROTEIN BASED GREASE - OFFAL

11,000 PEOPLE FALL IN RESTAURANTS EVERY DAY IN AMERICA.

©2024 RESTAURANT EXPERT WITNESS

An Introduction to Slip & Falls in America's Restaurant Industry

FALLS ARE A major cause of injury – and death – in this country and are "the second leading cause of accidental death and disability after automobile accidents" (The Bureau of Labor Statistics, 2020).

While some falls just can't be avoided, most of them can be and therefore the majority are preventable. Falls can happen almost anywhere – at home, at work, at the grocery store and even when you go out for a nice meal to one of your favorite or least favorite restaurants.

Unfortunately, going out to eat at a restaurant – which is such a major part of our culture and society today – is also the most likely place for you to suffer a slip and fall injury.

There are more slip and fall incidents in the restaurant industry than in any other industry doing business across this country. Slip and falls "are the number one cause of accidents in hotels, restaurants and public buildings according to the Bureau of Labor Statistics" (Willis).

In fact, "more than three million food service employees and over one million restaurant industry guests are injured annually because of slips, trips, and falls in America's restaurants. According to the National Floor Safety Institute (NFSI), the hospitality industry spends over $2 billion on such injuries each year; and these injuries are increasing at a rate of about ten percent annually."

This is Certainly No Laughing Matter

Do you remember the 70's sitcom "Three's Company"?

As a kid, I loved that show and I remember tuning in every Tuesday night to see what predicament – and how many slip and falls – the main character Jack Tripper would get himself into (the irony of the character's last name being Tripper wasn't lost on me as a child, either – after all I was reasonably bright for my age).

Played by the amazing late actor and pratfall comedian extraordinaire John Ritter, Jack would run into things, be hit by things, and/or fall down in a way that was invariably funny to me and millions of other Americans. We also had Dick Van Dyke and Chevy Chase back in the day as well as they used their similar brand of pratfall comedy to make audiences laugh in a wide variety of television shows, stand-up routines, and movies.

When people see actors slipping and falling on TV shows and movies – if it's pulled off just right – they are funny, because no matter how deep in the show you become, there's still a part of you that knows that the show isn't real and therefore neither is the fall, or the hurt. But in the real world – slips, trips, and falls are certainly no laughing matter.

Falls Can Hurt Your Bottom…and A Restaurant's Bottom Line

"Slips, trips, and falls account for… 39% of all general liability claims in the restaurant industry…"

"…For slips, trips, and falls, the average general liability claim cost for restaurants is $3,550. …the National Restaurant Association [reveals that] slips, trips and falls are the single largest cause of Emergency Room visits... cause over 20,000 fatalities in North America each year and are a leading cause of death in the workplace (second only to traffic accident fatalities)" (Judi, 2020) and it costs restaurants "tens of billions of dollars per year from regulatory fines, productivity losses, and other administrative expenses." (Society Insurance, 2021).

The financial loss to restaurants from slip and fall incidents not only comes from lawsuit losses, settlement claims, and workers' compensation claims, but also the loss of customers and billions of dollars in workers compensation matters and lost time from work.

"According to a survey of more than 1,000 Americans, nearly one in three adults – or 60 million Americans – are unlikely to visit a restaurant if they found out someone had slipped or fallen recently." (XpressMats, 2023).

Slip and Falls and Premises Liability

Slip and fall lawsuits are usually referred to as "premises liability" lawsuits.

"Premises liability is a legal responsibility imposed on the property owner due to injuries caused by unsafe conditions. An attorney bases the premises liability lawsuit on negligence. However, simply because the victim is injured on someone's property, it does [not] mean that the property owner is negligent." (Cloudlex, 2023).

And the premises are not limited to just inside the dining room either. "Slips, trips, and falls can happen in the dining room, kitchen, buffet area, parking lot, entryway, restroom, stairways—anywhere on the premises."

As an example, In January 2007, a New Jersey man "suffered spine and shoulder injuries after slipping on an untreated patch of ice near a storm drain in an unlit area of the restaurant's parking lot." The man – a single father of two – "sustained multiple disc herniations in his lower back and later underwent spinal fusion surgery to have various pieces of hardware implanted in the lower regions of his spine." (New Jersey Herald, 2011) In 2011, he was awarded 1.9 million dollars against the restaurant owners.

"The most common type of premises liability claim, by far, is a slip and fall or trip and fall...(One) in 10 lawsuits are related to premises liability. Premises liability victims are paid about $4 billion per year, but only 6% of cases feature punitive damages, which are often large amounts that inflate case value. The median settlement or verdict for premises liability lawsuits is around $45,000 but can reach $90,000. In cases where discs are damaged, herniated, bulging, or similar, the median climbs to $150,000" (Downtown LA Law Group, 2023)

The Laundry List of Restaurant Lawsuits

There are some slip and fall settlements where the victim is awarded a large settlement in the millions of dollars, based on the extent of the injuries or the blatant carelessness of the establishment.

Here's just a few examples:

- A Florida man was awarded 5.3 million dollars in 2022

after slipping and falling in a pizza restaurant. The store had "an overflowing grease trap (which) leaked onto the main floor. When the 24-year-old man and his daughter were leaving the restaurant, he slipped and fell on the grease, resulting in a 3mm disc protrusion at L3-4 and eventually requiring a lumbar laminectomy." (Morgan & Morgan, 2023).

- In 2019, a Texas man visited a Houston fast-food chain restaurant and while inside, "the man slipped and fell in a liquid substance that had accumulated on the floor. Apparently, at least one of the (restaurant's) employees was aware of the dangerous condition because the manager on duty told the employee to clean it up prior to the time the incident occurred. Despite knowledge of the dangerous condition presented by the liquid substance on the floor, the (restaurant's) employees made no attempt to warn invitees, including the man, of the dangers presented by the liquid substance. Moreover, despite knowledge of the dangerous condition, the (restaurant's) employees failed to follow through with appropriate mitigating measures such as cleaning the floor and setting out a wet floor sign to alert customers. The fall caused the man to sustain serious bodily injuries." He filed a lawsuit against the restaurant seeking "monetary relief for damages resulting from, among others, medical expenses both past and future, physical pain and suffering both past and future, and mental anguish, among others." (Wike, 2020).

- In 2007, a Texas woman was visiting her sister in Maui, Hawaii. She, her husband and her family were dining at a well-known fast-food restaurant, and she got up from her seat to get everyone drinks. She slipped on the floor and fell, falling "on her buttocks, which caused a burst compression fracture of the L1 vertebra in her lower back." (Daranciang, 2010). It was determined that restaurant management "did not follow safety rules for an extended period which caused a greasy film to form on the floor. On the day of the slip and fall accident, a 'food contaminant' was spilled on top of the already dirty floor and not cleaned up, according to mauinews.com." (Sharp Blog, 2017). She "underwent two surgeries, but all they did was stabilize the injury. She is now permanently disabled, suffers chronic pain and is confined to a wheelchair most of the time. The U.S. District Court jury awarded Munguia $2.67 million in special damages for past and future medical expenses, lost wages and retirement benefits. The jury also awarded her $3 million in general damages for pain, suffering and loss of enjoyment of life." (Daranciang, 2010).

There are countless others, including many that I have been involved in as a testifying expert, but you get the picture. These incidents aren't just little accidents an establishment can write off and sweep under the rug. They're unnecessary, brutal, and life-changing catastrophes that result in busted and broken backs, hips, butts, and bank accounts.

Customers Beware, But Also Employees Be Wary

Guests are not the only ones injured from slip and fall injuries in restaurants - employees often get injured as well.

The National Floor Safety Institute (NFSI) states that "slips and falls are the leading cause of workers' compensation claims." (NFSI). Sometimes it goes far beyond just a worker's compensation claim and the employee files a lawsuit.

For example, an Asian-style restaurant in Texas was ordered to pay over $100,000 in damages to a cook who slipped and fell "on his way to get soup from a cooler to prepare for a customer, causing immediate pain to his head and neck and leading to several other conditions that left him unable to work." (Business Insurance, 2020).

America, We Have a Problem

You can now see that slip and fall incidents – especially in restaurants – happen often. In fact, they happen as often as eight times per minute. And that is just in America's restaurants. The world-wide global numbers are even shockingly more.

They result in lost money for establishments and companies through worker's compensation claims, downtime of employees, lawsuit payouts, and even loss of customers; cause injuries which are sometimes life-changing and catastrophic; and at times can even cause loss of life.

Let me just re-emphasize how large and widespread a problem this is to try to help you see the size and significance of this issue.

More than four million people a year – over three million restaurant employees and one million restaurant guests – are injured in slip and fall accidents in America alone. To put that into perspective, as there are twelve months in a year, that's approximately 333,333 people injured a month. We'll just use a 30-day month and say that's approximately 11,111 people injured per day – 11 thousand per *day* – in a slip and fall incident in a restaurant in America.

If you wanted to break it down even further, that's approximately 463 people an hour and around eight people per minute.

So approximately eight people a minute across the United States are injured – some catastrophically – in restaurants.

Every minute. Every hour. Every day. Now, do you see how big the problem is?

But what really causes this? And what can be done to change things?

Well, I'm glad you asked. Several things really so let's keep plugging along.

The Coefficient of Friction Isn't a Lawsuit's Silver Bullet

Most lawyers want to argue that the coefficient of friction is the main cause of slip and falls in restaurants. But that's not going to be enough to win the argument or the case.

"The coefficient of friction is a numerical value describing the resistance an object will be under as it tries to slide across a surface. It is the ratio of the force required to slide it along a flat surface to the normal force on the object. If there are other vertical forces acting on the object, the normal force will not equal the object's weight." (Study.com, 2023).

Did your eyes roll back in your head just now reading that?

Maybe a better way for me to of explain that is "ice on steel has a low coefficient of friction – the two materials can slide past each other easily – while rubber on pavement has a high coefficient of friction – the materials do not slide past each other easily." (Science Direct, 2010).

A classic comparison is rubber to pavement – you are walking across a parking lot in your rubber-soled shoes, and you shuffle your feet or step wrong – your shoe does not slide easily against the pavement in this specific instance and therefore you stumble and fall. That is not a slip but instead a trip, a stumble, or a stub. Yes – those are all different things.

There was a high coefficient of friction between your shoe and the pavement – which many lawyers will try to use as the main reason for slips and falls in restaurants. But the coefficient of friction – even though it sounds very technical and official – is not the main culprit here.

Contributing Factors to Slip and Falls

There are many things that contribute to a slip and fall, but not all factors are created equal.

Of course, there are other things such as spills on the floor of liquids or food, freshly mopped floors or improperly used floor cleaner that becomes slick that can all contribute to slip and falls in restaurants. According to the Liberty Mutual Research Institute for Safety, "most same-level falls are the result of slipperiness caused by faulty housekeeping or defects of the floor surface. Faulty housekeeping is described as dirt, grease, water or contaminates of some sort on the floor, and defective floors are described as slippery floor dressings or finishes, inappropriate floor surface materials for the environment, surface wear and uneven or damaged surfaces." (Liberty Mutual Research Institute for Safety, 2002).

So, we have a problem, and the coefficient of friction isn't the main culprit in every instance…so what *is* the main culprit in many of these catastrophic cases?

I'm glad you asked that too.

CHAPTER 1
The Secret Sauce to These Cases: Offal

THE LARGEST AND *most important cause of slip and falls in restaurants is offal – protein-based grease.*

Offal?!?

Yes – offal.

So, you've never heard of it?

Webster's Dictionary defines offal as "the waste or by-product of a process: such as trimmings (such as the belly, head, and shoulders) of a hide; the by-products of milling (as of wheat or barley) used especially for stock feeds; the viscera and trimmings of a butchered animal removed in preparing it for market or for consumption."

However, while most just associate offal with animal entrails or guts, "offal refers to something that has fallen or been cast away from some process of preparation or manufacture" (Merriam-Webster Dictionary, 2023).

In this case, the "something that has been cast away" is the protein-based grease that is released when meat – any meat – is cooked in a restaurant. The steam from the cooking meat gets into the air and that steam contains protein-based grease – and it must go somewhere. It doesn't matter if the meat is cooked on a grill, in an oven, on a stove, in a fryer, or otherwise – the grease is unavoidable. In the restaurant industry we also use the term offal when it comes to the cooking greases that we use whether it be canola oil, peanut oil, vegetable oil, oily meat-based broths, and all other types and kinds of oils and greases coming from the proteins, the cooking, and the cooking processes.

It is why the restaurant industry has such things as grease traps, grease collection devices, Ansul systems for grease fires, and odor collection systems.

When meat and other food products get cooked, the grease gets into the air and becomes a light mist. It settles on the floor and hardens very quickly, becoming sticky. Most of the time, the layman rarely recognizes it or realizes that there is indeed grease on the floor – at least not until that moment when the slightest bit of moisture comes and rehydrates the oil - and then the flooring surface the employees and the customers are walking on becomes an ice-skating rink.

To give you an example to wrap your head around, think of men's hair gel. When it first gets applied it comes out of the container wet and slick and then after it has set for a few minutes it hardens. The dude can go all day, and his hair stays perfectly firm and in place. But then when he adds just a few drops of water the hair gel gets re-hydrated, and the stuff becomes slick and slippery all over again.

The protein-based grease, cooking greases, and offal that settle on the flooring surface of a restaurant act the exact same way. Over time it gets hardened on the flooring surface and is sitting in wait can be rehydrated by a number of factors or events that can thereby re-hydrate it and turn it back to its wet, slick, slippery, and dangerous self once again. This could include employees or customers walking inside from rain or snow, condensation dripping off a "sweating" glass, drips from a wet towel, condensation from a cold salad or dessert bowl being brought into a warmer environment, sunlight coming through a window that melts the hardened grease, drips from a faucet in the kitchen or restroom, water dripping from wet hands from using a hand dryer instead of towels, and even urine itself in the restroom (yes, even the restroom can be a hazard because the grease gets in the air and the entire building shares ventilation and therefore air).

There is a plethora of other ways the grease can turn from dormant and hardened to a slip and fall hazard as well.

The National Floor Safety Institute (NFSI) states that "most slips and falls that occur in the foodservice industry are directly caused by wet or otherwise dangerous floors." (The National Floor Safety Institute, 2003).

This is more likely than not going to be a critical factor for any lawyer to understand in their restaurant industry slip and fall case – so let us dig into it a little further.

Polymerization and Offal

"Grease, in the presence of water, can produce a very slippery floor. Over time, triglyceride molecules can unite to form a long chain polymer (called polymerization) and form a hard grease film on floors, resistant to most detergents.

Cleaning a restaurant kitchen floor with a mop and pail with hot water and detergent only partially cleans the floor." (Liberty Mutual Group, 2005). In fact, cleaning the floor improperly can actually make the floor even more unsafe. "Improper cleaning leaves dirt and soap residues on floors. This causes polymerization that turns otherwise safe floors into skating rinks, especially when the floor is wet. Sunlight and certain cleaning chemicals such as bleach and ammonia can make the problem worse by hardening the dirt and soap residue and sealing it in to the floor's surface." (New Pig, 2023).

"A restaurant kitchen floor is only clean when the polymerized grease film is also removed which means a suitable amount of detergent applied to the floor in 160-degree water with a dwell time period followed by a vigorous deck brushing." (Liberty Mutual Group, 2005).

I could go on for hours here alone, but I will save you the long boring details and just say that grease on floors, especially grease that has become polymerized, is not easy to get rid of and requires a reasonable and customary level of training, focus, effort, attention to detail, and oversight to resolve.

Injury Prevention Should Be Preventable

What is really sad is that nearly every injury in a restaurant – that changes or even ends someone's life – could have likely been avoided by following basic industry standard safety protocols for getting and keeping grease off of the floor.

Slips and falls in restaurants often lead to catastrophic injuries with things like broken femurs, broken hips or the person ending up in a wheelchair. They can be life-altering incidents and injuries for sure.

This is obviously a large, costly and dangerous problem for the restaurant industry. But it is not a problem that can't be solved. The solution is returning to the restaurant industry standards that are already in place. While preventing every single slip and fall incident and accident in any establishment is unlikely – employees, managers, owners, risk managers, and executives should always have zero tolerance, zero defects, and zero incidents as their goal.

Getting Back to Basics

There are restaurant industry standards for keeping floors hazard-free for the safety of guests and employees. These standards are and should be the norm, rather than the exception.

Over time, however, many restaurants quit making safety standards, risk management, and quality operational procedures, as a priority and have sadly decided to just not bother. They then end up paying for that negligence out of their bottom line by paying big dollars to lawyers and insurance claims and instead prefer that the victims pay for the ignorance and apathy of the restaurant managers and employees with their own pain and suffering.

The basic restaurant industry standards, policies, procedures, and protocols for cleaning and maintaining floors that should be done every single operational day include the following:

- Sweep the floor with a dry broom to remove debris and then rinse the floor with hot water.

- Mop the floor with a degreaser in a figure eight motion. Best results will be achieved with the use of a bio-enzymatic cleaner and degreaser. Grease is an organic soil, meaning it comes from something living. Grease is best removed with the use of bio-enzymatic cleaner and degreaser. To remove grease, bacteria in the cleaner and degreaser produces several enzymes that break up the grease. Then the bacteria in the cleaner eats the broken-down waste as a food source.

- Rinse the floor again with hot water.

- Add the floor cleaner and mop the floor with a clean mop in a figure eight motion. "Using a clean mop and bucket is critical to ensuring you are not re-soiling your floors during the cleaning procedure. A previously soiled mop will spread grease and oils around, further intensifying the slipperiness of floors." (Imperial Dade Insights Blog, 2019).

- It is important to give the degreaser and the cleaner time to dwell (sit) so that it can do what it is designed to do and infuse itself into the grease, grime, and dirt and separate the particles.

- Rinse the floor again with hot water.

- Use a deck brush to clean the floor surface at every stage a mop is used and before a final rinse and dry mop. Deck brushes are "tough scrubbing brushes on long handles. Not only can you use them to clean decking, but they're also great for giving almost any hard floor a really good scrub without having to get down on your hands and knees." (KDVR Fox 31, 2021).

- Give the floor a final rinse with hot water.
- Dry the floor with a dry mop and use fans to dry if it is deemed necessary.

OSHA Guidelines

Not only are there restaurant industry standards for keeping floors clean to mitigate the chances of slip and falls, but there are also restaurant specific guidelines put in place by OSHA, the Occupational Safety and Health Administration:

- OSHA, Walking-Working Surfaces Standard, General requirements section 1910.22(a)(2) - states the following: The floor of every workroom shall be maintained in a clean and so far as possible a dry condition. Where wet processes are used, drainage shall be maintained, and false floors, platforms, mats or other dry standing places should be provided where practicable.
- Sections 1910.22(a)(3) – 1910.22(b)(2) state: To facilitate cleaning, every floor, working place, and passageway shall be kept free from protruding nails, splinters, holes or loose boards. . .. Aisles and passageways shall be kept clear and in good repairs,

with no obstruction across or in aisles that could create a hazard. Permanent aisles and passageways shall be appropriately marked.

The Following Recommendations, Among Others, Should Be Implemented:

- Select floor cleaning and maintenance products with proven slip resistance characteristics that are compatible with the particular flooring surfaces in your facility. [Note: The National Floor Safety Institute states that 10 out of the 18 products that they tested that were approved for tile floor cleaning actually made the tile floors more slippery after they were cleaned using the product.]

- Provide proper signage and equipment to be used as a warning system during floor maintenance and quick reference for cleanup operations, such as safety cones, wet-floor signs, safety data sheets (SDS), and specifications regarding the slip-resistance level of products, safety posters, etc. [Note: OSHA's poster informing employees of their rights and responsibilities must be posted in a prominent location at all times to be in compliance and to meet industry standard.]
- Implement carpet runners and mats that adhere to

OSHA and ADA (Americans with Disabilities Act) guidelines.

- Consider foreseeable conditions, such as the weather (rain, mud, dirt, sand, snow, etc.); provide employee access to slip resistant footwear and make it a requirement; and
- Provide regular site safety and health inspections.

OSHA also recommends keeping the following in mind when selecting cleaning products:

- Detergents or surfactants: increase penetration of water-soluble soils and contaminants.
- Emulsifiers, soaps and degreasers: help to dissolve and suspend fat-soluble soils (using too little will be insufficient for removing grease; using too much may dissolve the grease but leave a slippery residue behind).
- Biological agents: blend naturally occurring bacteria with powerful enzymes for efficient, effective, safe cleaning, and removal of excessive grease.
- Caustics and acids (harsh or corrosive agents): chemically break down and strip contaminants.
- Other additives and agents (for slip-resistance, shining, sealing, fragrance, drying, and disinfectants): can help to minimize the chances of slip and falls.
- Clean mops are most effective; mops can become

contaminated quickly and spread grease and soil instead of removing it.

It is restaurant industry standard to:

- Use clean mops; replace, remove or thoroughly clean dirty mops (refer to the manufacturer for best cleaning instructions).
- Utilize dirt screens or water contaminate-separating agents for cleaner water in the mop bucket(s).
- Utilize several mop buckets to have separate compartments for dirty mop wringing, dirty mop rinsing, and cleaning solution dipping (floor squeegees may be used to spread cleaning solution to help minimize cross-contamination).

There are also proper procedures for washing restaurant floors for safety, as recommended by OSHA:

- Always choose the best time to clean (when other employees, customers, etc. are not around — unless, of course, you are cleaning up a spill) to allow for longer periods of drying time and the least chance that someone might slip or fall on the wet, freshly washed flooring surface.
- Set up appropriate warning/caution signage to keep others away while washing floors.
- Provide safe access around the work area when others are present.

- Prior to washing the floor, remove excess dirt or grease by wiping, scraping and/or sweeping (this makes cleaning easier and helps reduce the likelihood of contaminants from spreading).
- Avoid contacting surrounding restaurant equipment and machinery with water, cleaning agents, cleaning tools, and equipment.
- Use only the designated tools and cleaning materials for the particular area/zone of the restaurant that you are currently cleaning (check for labels and color codes).

- Rinse floors after scrubbing.
- Use a wet vacuum, floor machine or squeegee to force excess liquids into floor drains and speed up the drying process.
- Clean smaller areas/sections of the floor at a time for easier, more manageable clean up and to prevent cross-contamination.
- Start by cleaning the less soiled/contaminated areas; finish that area first, then proceed to the next dirtiest until complete (be sure to keep drainage in mind).

Employee Training Pertaining to Floors

OHSA and its affiliate organizations take employee training seriously. So should restaurants.

OSHA Safety & Health Program Management Guidelines state the following in regard to training: "Employee training programs should be designed to ensure that all employees understand and are aware of the hazards to which they may be exposed and the proper methods for avoiding such hazards. Supervisors should be trained to understand the key role they play in job site safety and to enable them to carry out their safety and health responsibilities effectively."

- **OSHA Employer responsibility; 1926.21(b)(2):** The employer shall instruct each employee in the recognition and avoidance of unsafe conditions and the regulations applicable to his work environment to control or eliminate any hazards or other exposure to illness or injury.

In addition to being recommended by OSHA, as well as ISSA (The Worldwide Cleaning Industry Association), and Alliance (an OSHA Cooperative Program), it is restaurant industry standard to implement, enforce and train the best safe practices, including, but not limited to, the following:

- Identify and correct (minimize, eliminate) possible slip and fall hazards.
- Report to management any blind corners, problems with floor surfaces or hazardous areas.
- Provide absorbent rags, mops, and squeegees to allow workers to clean up spills quickly to prevent falls.

- Provide adequate authority and resources to responsible parties.
- Provide industry standard facility management and equipment maintenance.
- Select high-traction, slip-resistant flooring materials.
- Use non-skid waxes and surfaces coated with grit to create non-slip surfaces in slippery areas or use non-slip mats.
- Know the slip-resistance of flooring materials; have flooring coefficient of friction (COF) audits performed regularly and consistently.
- Provide non-slip matting in areas that tend to be wet. (Some types of matting may not be effective in areas that tend to be greasy. The use of non-skid waxes and floor surfaces coated with grit may be helpful in these areas).
- Designate specific tools and cleaning materials for use in only certain areas/zones (label or color code them accordingly), such as "for fryer areas only," "Front of the House (FOH) only," and "Back of the House (BOH) only."

  o **FOH**: covers areas of exposures, such as outside curbs, ramps, parking stalls; entrance foyers (and to-go area); central walkways and aisles; dining, banquet rooms, bar and restrooms; elevated areas, steps and ramps.

o **BOH**: covers areas of exposure, such as the kitchen; dish/sink areas; expo line, cook line and prep areas; walk-in coolers and freezers; storage rooms; beverage stations; ice makers; stairs; and, back dock, trash and receiving areas.

The Little Things Matter in Restaurant Safety

Although employers cannot mandate proper foot attire for restaurant customers or visitors, restaurant employees should wear non-slip shoes (or use non-slip shoe covers) and avoid wearing sandals or open-toe shoes, high heels, or shoes made of canvas.

This is especially important when doing wet processes or greasy tasks such as spraying down parking lots or mopping floors. Employers implementing a shoe policy program may fund proper footwear. To ensure that the proper footwear and safety precautions are implemented, employees should remember:

- Lace and tightly tie their shoes.
- Avoid leather or smooth soles.
- Do not wear open-toed shoes.
- Avoid porous fabrics such as canvas – they do not provide enough protection and still slip. Besides that, hot liquids, if spilled on canvas, would easily burn through the canvas and burn one's feet.

Besides the shoes, there are some other general, common-sense practices in keeping the floors safe overall.

- Do not wear pants or clothing that are over-sized, baggy or extended below shoe level, causing a potential hazard.

- Do not run or move too quickly so to create a dangerous condition.

- Do not store items on the floor that might be slipped or tripped on – especially hot cooking oil because someone may slip and fall into it as well.

- Carry items only at a height that you can safely see over.

- Keep passageways and walkways sufficiently wide for easy movement, free of clutter and crowding, clear and in good repair with no obstruction across or within aisles that could create a hazard (for example, provide floor plugs for equipment to avoid power cords running across aisles and pathways).

- Keep floors clean and dry (in addition to being a slip hazard, surfaces that are continually wet promote the growth of mold, fungi and bacteria that can cause infections).

- Clean up spills. During rush periods or peak traffic periods, spot mopping (cleaning only the immediately affected area of the spill) is the safest and most effective method to clean (floor pads or towels may work as well).

- Provide adequate drainage; and for wet processes, maintain drainage (replace any loose drain covers); keep grates/drains free from debris and blockage; provide false floors, platforms, mats or other dry standing places where practicable.

- Decrease overcrowding by adding additional supply stations or carts with supplies at convenient locations.

- Provide adequate lighting, especially in serving and preparation areas.

- Alert employees and guests to step-ups and step-downs by using hazard tape or other warning signs.

- Provide mirrors for blind corners.

- Provide windows on swinging doors so you can see if someone is coming out. Also, provide two-way doors — one for only going in and one for only coming out.

- Follow a set traffic pattern to avoid collisions (for example, enter on the right side, exit on the left);

- Use signage on doors.

- Keep all places of employment clean and orderly and in a sanitary condition.

- Provide warning signs for wet floor areas and when mopping.

- Keep exits free from obstruction; access to exits must remain clear of obstructions at all times.

- Repair any uneven floor surfaces;

re-lay or stretch carpets that bulge or have become bunched to prevent hazards.

- Do not overfill bussing containers (in addition to causing strain injuries from lifting, overfilling creates the potential danger of spills and items falling out — not only posing a hazard for slip and falls, but also causes distractions for those carrying the containers who may be trying to focus on keeping the items from falling).

- Use safety gear (personal protective equipment — PPE) to protect eyes, face, skin, and feet.

- Inform employees of the dangers of mixing certain chemicals.

Consider the Catastrophe of Slip and Falls

Slip and falls can be funny and entertaining when they are part of some slapstick comedy sketch or an online video of failures and flubs. But not when someone breaks their tailbone right in front of their family while trying to enjoy a meal out on the town.

We've all seen those slow-motion videos capturing the funny falls and fails of someone letting go of the rope swing a bit too early or awkwardly, and ending up face planting into the dirt just inches short of a lake. Or the novice skier that loses a bit of control going down the slippery slope and sliding into the bushes that are a few feet off the ended course.

I will even be the first to admit and be fully transparent that, even though I know I should not find humor in these things, I can't help but sometimes love getting a good laugh when someone splits their pants or eats it slipping on a banana peel – and besides I'm pretty sure they were all scripted for our entertainment... right?!?

But a slip and fall in a restaurant is nothing like any of those. It is real and often times catastrophic and even life changing for everyone involved. And *thousands of these events happen in restaurants across America every single day.* As the frequency of these incidents and accidents continues to climb and the negative impact on people's lives and bank accounts across the country and around the world climbs with it, it's clear that this is no laughing matter.

I would imagine that most of the readers of this book will be attorneys, risk managers, insurance adjusters and executives, restaurant owners and managers, and those that have been injured by a slip and fall in a restaurant or bar.

As you have hopefully been able to see, my goal and objective has been to give you some insight into slip and falls that take place in restaurants, bars, food, and beverage industry establishments, as well as a better understanding of the industry recognized hazards, risks, operational systems, and preventive measures.

Obviously, I can't provide everything there is to share about this subject matter in one book as time and space is limited. But my hope is that the material contained within this book has been valuable to you so far and will continue to be through the next hundred or so pages.

Are You Advocating on Behalf of Someone Who Has Suffered a Life-Altering Slip or Fall Incident in a Restaurant or Bar?

I understand that this book is not Hemingway or Shakespeare. To be fair, it's not based on a subject matter that is all that entertaining or enjoyable to read. I know that and so do you. However, it is vital information for you if you are an attorney dealing with these types of legal matters in state or federal court.

It is also crucially important information for those working in the restaurant or bar industry as general managers, assistant managers, shift managers, risk managers, owners, multi-unit managers, and company executives, all of whom have a purview of responsibility for the safety, health, and security of people and premises.

If you're an insurance provider with restaurant and bar industry clients, you need the information contained in this book as well.

If you or a loved one has already experienced a slip and fall incident, the information contained in this book will be especially helpful to you as well. However, if this is the case, I would highly recommend retaining a practicing, qualified, and professional attorney to handle everything for you, as this will ensure that you have the best possible representation. Without an experienced lawyer to represent you, you risk being uninformed and overwhelmed by the court system. You risk missing out on the maximum care and award for damages due to you and you will get the short end of the stick. Please trust me on that.

I can tell you from experience that one of the biggest challenges I face with these types of legal matters, and when dealing with attorneys, insurance carriers, plaintiffs, and defendants, is slowing everyone down long enough to get them to listen.

This is what I am constantly trying to get them to hear, "Slip and falls that take place in any restaurant, bar, or food and beverage industry establishment are completely different from slips and falls that take place in any other industry."

This is so important that I feel it is necessary for me to repeat it. *Slip and falls in restaurants are completely different from slips and falls in any other industry.*"

Now, you need to know why. Slip and falls in restaurants can be caused by any number of factors, not the least of which is the restaurant industry specific recognized hazard "offal", cooking oils, or protein-based greases that we have already discussed.

This stuff called offal, cooking oils, or protein-based grease and the restaurant industry specific policies, procedures, standards, operating systems, safety rules, and tools of the trade that must be used to handle and gain victory over it is the glaring, substantial, and significant difference between the restaurant, bar, food and beverage industry and everyone else. There are several other industry specific factors that we will also dig into further throughout the pages of this book, but for now that's all you need to know, until you keep reading.

Quite honestly, I can't completely let the cat out of the bag just yet, especially if I want you to read the whole book, which I certainly do. Besides, it's this stuff called offal, cooking oils, and protein-based greases, along with the industry specific standards, training, operating protocols, and management oversight that go along with it (or the lack thereof) that, since 1987, have provided me with such a financially lucrative career. Sad but true.

Simply stated, many of those in charge of the premises at both the unit and the corporate levels, from operations to risk management, and from safety to human resources, have stunk up the joint (literally, figuratively, and financially) because of the hazards, secrets, and dangerous conditions I'm revealing throughout this book and have been revealing in court cases from sea to shining sea for several decades now.

Greasy floors lead to more slip and fall incidents and accidents which lead to more litigation matters – which lead to my business booming more and more each year. In full disclosure – greasy floors lead to me getting more cases and making more money.

But I would still rather the floors not be greasy and find other kinds of work to get paid for.

Who am I and Why am I Qualified as an Expert?

Now is probably a good time as any for me to tell you a little bit about myself to establish my credibility so that you can know that my words have value for you. In 1987, I started Restaurant Operations Institute, Inc. My brands, ROI, Inc and Restaurant Expert Witness, are well-known in the restaurant and bar industry, across the country, and around the globe. My entire career has been dedicated specifically to the restaurant and bar industry.

I am an author of several books, an industry speaker, consultant, forensic scientist, and a court testifying expert witness for state and federal lawsuits and insurance claims. My areas of expertise include risk management, safety, and operational execution specific to restaurants and bars. In fact, my only areas of study, research, and expertise over these last thirty-seven years has been the restaurant and bar industry, and – over the last seven years – the Bible. I was saved by the Grace of God in 2017.

My books have been published in 76 countries around the globe and in several different languages. I am the author of The Complete Idiot's Guide to Starting a Restaurant (First and Second Editions) and Restaurant OSHA Safety & Security – The Book of Restaurant Industry Standards & Best Practices – as well as other Titles.

At the time of this writing, I have more than 300 expert witness cases in state and federal courts and more than 350 pre-litigation projects and cases across the country and around the world to my credit. I have appeared on national television shows such as Dr. Oz, Anderson Cooper, Good Morning America, Inside Edition, CNN, Fox, NBC, the Travel Channel, and more, and I have done work in every state of the United States as well as dozens of countries around the globe.

My primary areas of industry specific expertise are slip and falls, coffee burns in fast food drive throughs, acts of violence including rapes, murders, and wrongful deaths, bar fights and negligent security, intentional food and beverage contaminations, and alcohol and dram shop matters.

I don't tell you any of this to try to impress you. I tell you this only to impress upon you that my entire career has been spent dealing with a truly extraordinary number of incidents, accidents, hazards, and events involving a mind-boggling number of restaurant industry policies, procedures, standards, operating systems, safety protocols, and legal matters that pertain specifically to the types of incidents that take place exclusively in the restaurant, bar, food and beverage industry.

Because of what I do for a living, I, like few others, have had the unique opportunity to witness and experience things pertaining to these kinds of matters like very few others that walk this earth. I have also spent most of my career, and much of my life for that matter, under oath to tell the truth, the whole truth, and nothing but the truth, so help me God.

Since I was saved by the grace of God a handful of years ago, I am now required to tell the truth, the whole truth, and nothing but the truth, so help me God, all the time – in both my personal and professional life. This is both because of the life I want to live with Jesus who I love so much, and because of the state and federal courts across the country that I desire to work in, and that I am required to offer my opinions under oath in.

Because of the strange and unique way that I happen to make my living, combined with the shocking, catastrophic, and life-altering incidents that take place in restaurants and bars around the world, I often find myself regularly smack-dab in the middle of these cases. Being that this is what I do, chances are good that I've got something for you that will alter your thinking, help you become more aware, and maybe even blow your mind a bit about something that seems as innocuous as a slip and fall in restaurant establishment.

No matter who you are, what you do, or what relationship your client has to a restaurant or bar, whether he or she works in one, manages one, owns one, breaks bread in one, knocks back a few cold ones in one, provides a product or service to one, insures one, defends one, sues one, dines in one – or has friends, family, or loved ones that do – they all, individually and collectively, deserve to be safe and secure when in one of America's and the world's restaurants or bars.

INSIDER SECRETS TO SLIP & FALLS IN RESTAURANTS

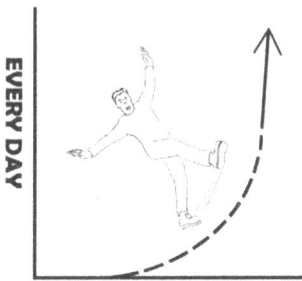

EVERY DAY

11,000 Slip & Falls happen
in US Restaurants

WHY?

Offal

Offal is a protien based
grease that comes from
cooking meat & using oils.

Offal releases into air
when cooking meat
& using oils.

Offal settles on the
floor as grease &
eventually hardens.

Offal then gets
rehydrated & becomes
dangerously slick.

Offal grease is the
leading cause of slip
& falls in restaurants.

CHAPTER 2
How It Usually Goes "Down" (Pun Intended)

N O ONE HEADS out to eat dinner with family and friends expecting to have their feet slide out from under them while simply walking across the dining room floor as they head to use the restroom. Not only is it embarrassing to be swept off your feet in this manner, and stressful for everyone in the party, but it usually brings the fun-filled evening of dining and entertainment abruptly to an end and instead makes for a long night hanging out in the emergency room.

Many of these events, where people slip and fall due to the presence of protein-based grease, are recognizable because of the level of the violent fall that they experience. These falls are often so intense and violent that it becomes much more than just your everyday slip and fall and instead becomes a life-altering for those that experienced it. Think of a one-hundred-pound bag of potatoes hitting the floor after being slammed straight down from eighty-seven feet in the air. A dead drop and a huge thud. Sure, maybe a tad bit of an overreach, but I wanted to be over-the-top with my descriptive comment to simply impact you with the violent nature of these types of falls.

Often, these incidents leave an indelible mark on everyone involved, especially the person hitting the floor, but also those that witness it. The sound. The hurt. The crying. The blood. The rattling of the windows. The loud and dull thump of human flesh and bones hitting the ground forever embedded into human memory. Maybe even try imagining a watermelon even – your skull and bones – hitting concrete. Graphic I know, but that is what happens with staggering frequency across the restaurant and bar industry from sea to shining sea and all around the globe.

No one wants to think about this happening to them, but this type of incident or accident happens every single day in America's restaurants. In fact, events just like the one described above occur more than 11,000 times per day in US restaurants alone. I repeat this because it is that important. These are not here and there isolated incidents. The restaurant and bar industry in America experiences more slips and falls than all other industries combined.

It happens a lot. Many, many times a day.

You heard me right! More than four (4) million slip and falls happen in America's restaurants each year and millions more happen in restaurants and bars around the globe as well as aboard cruise ships, airplanes, in bowling alleys, casinos, hotels, sports stadiums, and the like – all kinds of places where foods and beverages are served.

Maybe you or someone you love hasn't taken a nosedive or dove a back-flop or hip-drop onto a dining room, bar, or bathroom floor ever… or lately. So maybe it's hard for you to wrap your head completely around it. Maybe you haven't personally experienced the fear, the anxiety, the embarrassment, or the pain that comes from one of these events or being placed on a gurney while customers and employees are hovering around you and watching the paramedics load you into the back of an ambulance. Maybe you haven't had to watch as your child, parent, or grandparent gets loaded and rushed off in a siren-blaring ambulance before you even have the chance to take your first bite of your entrée or finish your ice-cold beer.

Maybe you don't know the feeling when you hear for the first time that a near and dear member of your family, or one of your closest friends, will be spending the remainder of their earthly years confined to a wheelchair. Maybe you don't know or understand the excruciating pain that results from a serious back, hip, knee, or ankle injury caused by a seemingly simple slip and fall in a restaurant.

Well, you may not, but I can assure you that many do.

Remember the four (4) million injuries from slip and falls in America's restaurants and bars every year that I mentioned earlier? That number makes slips and falls the greatest cause of liability claims and lawsuits in US restaurants. And remember that 11,000 per day number that I shared with you? Well, tomorrow, or someday after, you could be one of those 11,000. You could be added to that statistic, or it could be someone near and dear to your heart: your wife, your husband, your mom or dad, your grandma or grandpa, child, or dear friend. Or maybe you're reading this book because it's already happened to you, or a loved one, or to one of your clients.

Perhaps you are a lawyer who is looking for answers to assist your client in winning a lawsuit or navigating the entire deal with the insurance carrier. Whatever the reason, I can almost certainly assure you that if you spend enough time in and around restaurants, you, or someone you know, will get injured, harmed, maimed, or killed from a slip and fall. The numbers suggest that it's bound to happen.

If you are a practicing attorney and if you practice in this sector of law long enough, you will most assuredly be involved with these types of cases involving plaintiffs and defendants whose slip and falls took place in one of America's restaurants or bars or other kind of food and beverage industry establishment.

My job here is to increase awareness of these types of

incidents, to provide some basic insight on how best to deal with them after something bad has happened, and, most importantly, how to hopefully prevent them from happening in the first place, as most of these incidents are preventable.

If you're going to understand slip and falls, it's important to understand how dangerous the entire restaurant industry is in the first place.

Restaurants are America's Most Dangerous Industry

"What's going on in America's restaurants?"

"I had no idea that restaurants could be this dangerous."

"What's the issue here?"

These are questions and comments I hear frequently in my line of work. The best answer I can give you to the question about what's going on in restaurants is that mediocrity, below industry standard performance, and outright management neglect is what leaves restaurants and bars vulnerable to lawsuits and customers at increased risk of injury or death.

The restaurant and bar industry, the industry that I so dearly love and have spent my entire career working in, is rife with incompetence, ignorance, apathy, and laziness. It would seem, based on the number of incidents, that a large percentage of owners and management-level personnel don't have enough drive, ambition, or sense of responsibility to fix it. Many of those placed in charge of restaurant and bar premises, and the employees that work for them, lack basic dangerous condition awareness, basic safety and security training, and basic day-to-day operational and risk management training and education.

But it goes beyond that.

Quality management competency and management oversight, in many instances, are nearly nonexistent.

Sadly, this cesspool of mediocrity and below industry standard level of performance is putting us all at risk.

But make no mistake about it, restaurant industry employees, at every level, regardless of compensation, do not wake up in the morning wanting to do a lousy job. It's the bad management to whom they report that inspires them to do that and puts them in that position. The alternative is also true. Managers who truly care provide great oversight and are focused on meeting the industry standards and providing consistent day-to-day operational performance that leads to inspired employees wanting to do a great job for their boss and for the families that they work with and serve.

No matter what anyone tells you, or wants you to believe, there is absolutely nothing wrong with the workers, the workforce, or this generation or workers. The problem lies with the owners and management; those who are supposed to be in charge. They want your money, but they aren't necessarily always willing to do the work the right way to get it. Of course, there are exceptions, many exceptions.

Based on what I do for a living, I'm sure that you fully understand that I can't name names of who is the most negligent or which restaurants I don't recommend you go to. You will need to conduct your own research. But I can tell you this; the superstar owners, managers, operations, brands, and establishments are obvious, at least to me, and so are those that are mediocre, and those that are clearly dangerous death traps.

There are plenty of great restaurants, restaurant owners and managers, and restaurant experiences. However, conversely, and sadly enough, the restaurant industry is also America's most dangerous industry. And quite frankly, the number two most dangerous industry isn't even all that close in garnering that number one spot.

The numbers speak loud and clear for themselves and even though many want to try to debate and argue this point, for mostly selfish reasons, the facts are the facts.

The truth, the whole truth, and nothing but the truth is this; more people get injured, harmed, sickened, maimed, or killed in America's restaurants and bars than they do in any other industry. Period.

You've probably never heard of most of these cases. Unless something of this nature happens in a restaurant or bar in your immediate area or happens to someone that you know personally, it is unlikely that you will hear about them in the future either.

So, why is it that you don't hear more about these types of incidents, accidents, catastrophic injuries, and deaths that happen in restaurants and bars? Why don't they appear in news headlines?

Those are great questions, and the answer is simple: Protective Orders.

Protective Orders and Confidentiality Agreements are put into place by attorneys, judges, and the courts for nearly every one of these types of cases to keep these matters quiet, confidential, and on the "down low", at least as much as reasonably possible.

This allows these legal matters to be discovered, negotiated, argued, settled, resolved, and, if necessary, tried, without any outside interference of public opinion or media outrage.

I call this the "not-so-public, public record."

Because of what I do for a living, I am privy to hard evidence, intimate details, and glorious and not-so-glorious aspects of these incidents that would blow your mind and shake you to your core.

I see firsthand the good, the bad, and the ugly of the industry that I love so deeply. I see the blood, the guts, the tears, the negligence, the lies and deceit, and the truth.

Restaurants are not just about hamburgers and French fries, grilled chicken and grits, or steak and potatoes. They're about people, and it's not just about the service and hospitality of people. It's about the safety, health, and security of people.

I don't say all of this to be dramatic either. I say this to help you understand that I have probably seen more policy and procedure manuals, more inner workings from more restaurant industry organizations and establishments – from the giant multi-billion dollar national and international chains to the single unit restaurant Mom and Pop independents – than probably anyone on the face of the earth.

Of course, I'm not allowed to share the details of any company or brand specific information. I cannot throw anyone under the bus, so to speak. I too am bound by Protective Orders and Confidentiality Agreements.

In fact, I must shred all my files at the conclusion of every case. But that doesn't mean I don't remember. I remember very well, in fact.

I remember the heartbreaking stories of the victims.

I remember the horrific pictures of those injured, harmed, sickened, maimed, and killed, the people, the events, the injuries, and the details, some of which will forever be etched in my mind. Quite honestly, I wouldn't wish those images and memories to be thrust on anyone else, ever. They are often horrific and disturbing. I even try to go so far as to protect my staff from having to see the gore and nastiness of it all, at least as much as I reasonably can.

I have handled some nasty, nasty cases over the years; cases that have changed people's lives forever. I've handled heartbreaking cases involving people from every walk of life, every demographic, and every age group, losing life and limb in restaurants and bars across America and around the world. Who would have ever thought – right?!?

To be fair, these matters aren't all peaches and cream for the restaurant and bar owners, managers, employees, or company executives either. They result in tens of millions of dollars in insurance claims, lawsuits, judgments, awards, damages, and citations.

The checkbooks get spread open wide and countless checks are written to attorneys, private investigators, and yes, forensic experts too.

In full disclosure, I get paid very well for doing what I do, and I am grateful to God for the provisions, but it also hurts my heart.

When my services are engaged, I am being asked to use my expertise and experience to provide only unbiased opinions to a reasonable degree of professional certainty about the incident, about the restaurant's standards, policies, procedures, and systems, about the participants and the specifics of the case and the testimony provided, and about the causes that led to the incident at the center of the underlying legal matter or claim.

An unbelievable number of man-hours are expended by lawyers, judges, paralegals, legal secretaries, court reporters, experts, and restaurant owners and managers on these cases. Those of us in the legal world are trained, educated, and developed to spend those countless hours toiling away with legal matters. Restaurant and bar owners, managers, executives, and employees – not so much. They would be better served spending time running their restaurants and bars rather than answering interrogatories, pulling together discovery documents, and making appearances at depositions and trials.

As you may know, making a profit in the restaurant industry is no easy task to begin with, so just imagine how difficult it becomes when those that are supposed to be running the restaurant, or group of restaurants, are left to dedicate hours and large sums of money to defending themselves, their business, their policies and procedures, their standards, their company culture, the actions of their employees, and their own actions.

Raising Awareness About Restaurants

More than anything, I am going to provide you with awareness and understanding, and hopefully enough information to help you be well on your way to winning your legal battle.

As I only have your attention for a limited amount of time, I can only provide you with so much information here. Obviously, these matters, and every lawsuit dealing with these types and kinds of matters, are highly complex.

If you are a practicing attorney it is my hope that the material in this book will help you put the pieces in place to improve your case on behalf of your client and determine what should have been done by the owner, manager, or supervisor of a restaurant.

If you are a restaurant industry employer, owner, or manager, this book is not necessarily directed towards you, but I believe this material will help you consider and reconsider what things need to be implemented at your restaurant or group of restaurants before someone gets injured, harmed, sickened, maimed, or killed on your watch.

Ignorance of restaurant industry standards and the safety and security rules and the laws of the land that go with them is not an acceptable excuse. But people don't know what they don't know…right?

That is one of the reasons that I decided to bring this information to you. I have grown weary of hearing people providing testimony at depositions or trials saying, "I don't know", when it is obvious to me that they certainly should know.

If I provide education, beyond just waiting for another multi-million-dollar lawsuit, I will more positively impact the industry, the people, and the world. I have felt called to step forward, not just stand back and do nothing. With that I have chosen to try to educate anyone that is willing to listen and learn.

For instance, did you know that anyone (in any capacity) who is placed in charge of managing employees, or the premises of a restaurant or bar, must provide competent person oversight to be compliant with industry standards and OSHA standards?

You may also not know that when a person is placed in charge, that person is instantaneously designated as a person who is supposed to be competent according to industry guidelines and standards, whether they or anyone else realizes it, or likes it, or not.

It's also true, and important to know, that such a designation comes with a significant amount of responsibility and a clear understanding of roles and responsibilities as it pertains to safety, health, and security.

Regardless of the level of training that person received (if any at all), he or she will be held accountable, as will their boss and the owner, if any incident happens while this person is in charge. This is what I call in the restaurant and bar industry the "all good, clean fun, until someone gets an eye poked out – or someone slips and falls and breaks open the back of their skull – concept."

Once someone gets injured, harmed, sickened, maimed, or killed, the fun stops and the person left in charge (and the person who decided to leave them in charge) will be scrutinized with a fine-tooth comb by a whole slew of lawyers, attorneys, and investigators. Trust me on that one. That's a big part of my job, in fact.

If that person does not operate according to what is considered the reasonable and customary industry standards, as it pertains to recognizing hazards and eliminating dangerous conditions, the restaurant business, the ownership, and the insurance carrier will be held responsible and will be "on the hook".

Once on the hook, the fun and games end, and everyone gets much more somber and straight-faced. That's when those in charge will have their feet held to the fire and be made accountable for their actions and behaviors that led up to that critical blow that caused someone to get their eye-poked out, or their butt busted, and their wallet blown open both figuratively and literally. Yes, I have had cases where people have had their eyes poked out in restaurants, too.

One of my most memorable cases dealt with a forty-something-year-old woman who leaned over a tabletop to get into a deep booth seat. She stuck herself in the eye with a unique (and dangerous) tabletop ornament that jabbed deep within her left eye-socket and completely eviscerated her eyeball. She was rushed to the hospital in the back of the ambulance while still holding the ornament with her eyeball squired and speared on top of it.

I have countless gory slip and fall stories I could tell here too, but I don't want to go down that rabbit hole just yet and figured the eye-ball story would do a good enough job of catching your attention. But enough of that for now.

Trust me when I say that I understand just how daunting safety rules, industry standards, company guidelines, OSHA codes, and risk management recommendations can be especially in environments where management personnel and ownership is not all that committed to safety and security. But it really does start with a culture being created where hazard awareness is high, and a culture of safety being created by management personnel that provides competent person oversight where the employees care about the safety, health, and security of themselves and others.

A culture of safety takes time and commitment and is not always the easiest thing to create and maintain in a restaurant or bar, especially if the highest level of people in charge of the joint aren't fully engaged and committed themselves. Again, remember, employees will follow the leaders.

And of course, providing the employees and other managers with the necessary consistent and continual flow of policies, procedures, standards, and guidelines requires a certain amount of time, money, and effort.

But…

The Sobering and Painful Truth

If current trends continue, more people than ever before will be injured, harmed, sickened, maimed, or killed on the premises of America's restaurants and bars this year, next year, and in the years to follow than ever before.

In an ever-growing litigious society, these kinds of incidents, accidents and events will lead to even more lawsuits and insurance claims filed against restaurants and bars, restaurant and bar owners, and of course, restaurant and bar insurance carriers.

Even more restaurant and bar owners, operators, managers, executives, and employees will have to spend more of their precious and valuable time defending themselves and their actions.

More and more money – millions and millions of dollars will be paid out to injured, harmed, sickened, maimed, and killed parties and their families than at any other time in our nation's and in our industry's history.

Perhaps, now is as good a time as any for me to provide you with some basic industry specific statistics that should give you a better understanding of what it is that I am talking about here and the glaring and shocking statistics staring us all right in the face – if we care to see them.

The Shocking Restaurant Industry Statistics

Every single year, thousands of employees, customers, and vendors die in America's restaurants. Yes, you heard that right! Thousands. Millions more will be injured, harmed, sickened, or maimed from a potpourri of different kinds of incidents, accidents, and events. The stats and facts speak for themselves and are loud and clear – even though they are often times highly difficult to track and get an exact bead on.

Please note the following statistics are constantly changing, sometimes easy to find and other times not so easy to find; sometimes come with conflicting numbers, and because this book will have a long lifespan, these are rough estimates rather than hard and firm numbers. This material is not being submitted to a court of law and, therefore, the statistics I am providing are general in nature and in some instances estimates and guesstimates and in other instances maybe simply pulled from thin air, mostly based on my experience and cannot necessarily be cited or fully reliable as a hard and fast stat. And because I don't have to in this forum, I'm not always providing research or citations herein.

Also, for impact and clarity purposes I will provide more than just slip and fall numbers and will delve slightly into other injuries and incidents as well as those industry stats or estimates.

That being said, somewhere between four to ten people will die today in America's restaurants. Another four to ten will die tomorrow, and the day after, and the day after that, and so on, and so on. The average number of deaths in America's restaurants and bars on any given day works out to be roughly eight – give or take.

Did you hear that?

Let me repeat it.

Eight people per day die in America's restaurants!

But it doesn't stop there.

Thirty people per day are raped in America's restaurants and bars!

The numbers worldwide are even more shocking, but, for

obvious reasons getting reliable numbers is very difficult, and often impossible.

Before this calendar year is out, thousands will be dead, and literally tens of thousands more will be severely injured, harmed, sickened, poisoned, and maimed from a record setting number of incidents, accidents, mishaps, miscues, screw-ups, and missteps that take place in restaurants across the land.

Slips, falls, rapes, murders, wrongful deaths, bar fights, robberies, chemical ingestions, coffee scalds, building explosions, gas leaks, electrical shortages, fires, cuts, burns, and a whole lot more will amount to a massive number of lawsuits and insurance claims of various types, sizes, and kinds.

Millions more, over 30 million in fact, which is well over 90,000 people a day, will become ill or sickened from ingesting restaurant and bar food and beverage, as well as grocery foods and beverages that were either toxic, unsafe for human consumption, or intentionally contaminated.

State and federal courts, as well as the offices and desks of lawyers, insurance adjusters, mediators, and arbitrators, have a mountain of files in an ever-expanding caseload of restaurant, bar, food, and beverage cases. And for that matter so do I.

My practice, Restaurant Expert Witness, can accept as many cases as I choose to take. The demand for my services is higher than ever before. Even though I continue to answer the phone and take on some of the cases, I'm in a season of life where I'm sickened by the sheer number of problems that persist in America's restaurants and bars that continue to lead to countless numbers of people being injured, harmed, sickened, raped, maimed, or killed. I have and continue to dial down my case load as I get closer to the end of my career, but the company itself is going to be in business long after I am gone.

Let's start by giving you a snapshot of the enormity of the restaurant, bar, food, and beverage industry first, and its incredible impact on our entire society and the American way of life.

- There are more than one (1) million restaurant industry establishments in the United States alone, with somewhere between 10,000 and 15,000 new restaurant and bar openings every year in markets across the country. These restaurants positively impact the economies in the marketplaces where they do business, unlike any other business sector really.

- There are more than fifteen (15)

million restaurant-industry employees, accounting for more than 11% of the entire US workforce.

- The industry boasts more than eight hundred (800) billion dollars in annual sales, which accounts for more than two (2) billion dollars in sales each day. It also accounts for a 47% share of the entire US food dollar spent by families across the country.

- More than 1.7 million new restaurant industry jobs are expected to be created over the next decade.

- Well over 150,000 vendors, suppliers, and product and service companies support the industry, adding millions of additional jobs to the workforce and billions of dollars to the US economy.

The restaurant industry is still one of America's greatest entrepreneurial opportunities and one of America's most reliable economic engines from coast to coast.

Okay, now that you've had a chance to digest that information, I will hit you with some of the bad and the ugly about the industry.

- Here's one I've already told you a few times but for clarity and depth of learning I will say it again: there are an estimated four (4) million slip and falls in America's restaurants every year. This includes both employees and customers. To put this number into proper perspective that means that somewhere between 10,000 to 12,000 slip and falls happen in restaurants and bars every single day in the United States alone. Many, many more happen world-wide.

- Sixty-eight (68%) percent of all US food-borne illness cases come from eating in restaurants. That is nearly thirty-three (33) million cases annually, with 3,000 of these cases resulting in someone dying. That's right. Stone cold dead! Not to be cold and insensitive, but rather to attempt to try to stop myself from getting teary-eyed from the heartache, and quite frankly in an effort to help you digest this information a bit better and understand the seriousness of it all – that does take the term "stick a fork in 'em" to an entirely different level don't you think?

- Thirty-three (33%) percent of all Equal Employment Opportunity Commission ("EEOC") sexual harassment claims come from the restaurant industry.

- Roughly forty (40) states have dram shop/alcohol liability laws placing the onus on owners, managers, bartenders, and servers to recognize visible intoxication in their customers and to determine the right time to cut someone off and determine whether or not the person is intoxicated or not simply by looking at them, and how best to help them safely leave the premises and get home without maiming or killing someone or themselves. Do I even have to tell you how dangerous drunk driving is? Well, apparently so, because still to this day, 20% of binge drinkers (defined as those that consume four to five drinks or more) drive drunk after leaving restaurants and bars, on a regular basis. Have you even considered how dangerous alcohol is, and the nasty role that alcohol has played in a wide variety of other incidents when someone gets injured, harmed, sickened, maimed, or killed on or off the premises of a restaurant or bar? I can tell you from my experience with these cases, many times it plays a leading role.

Millions of other employee and customer incidents, accidents, events, and mishaps take place in or revolve around America's restaurants and bars. Maybe I should share just a little bit about a few of them. Things like:

- Rapes, murders, wrongful deaths, and violent assaults in volumes that sicken me to even think about.
- Bar fights and intense brawls – many that are so brutal I can hardly wrap my head around people having that much pent-up anger and hate inside of them.
- Shootings and stabbings of all kinds and with an ever-expanding arsenal of weaponry.
- Alcohol-related incidents, accidents, and fatalities. I'm certain you are aware that the over-consumption of alcohol is killing us in countless ways, even if you don't want to admit it fully. You might even be knocking back a couple of cold ones while you're reading this book. I wouldn't blame you. I relaxed with one or two, here and there, while I was writing it but I see no reason to

get drunk really, or jump behind the wheel of a motor vehicle after I've been drinking.

- Thefts and robberies. Shockingly, 21% of all workplace robberies take place in restaurants and bars.

- Burns and scalds that are too many to track. For the obvious reason of having kitchens and serving hot foods and beverages, the restaurant industry has the highest burn and scald incident rate of any industry. But you might not have thought about hot coffee and hot tea burns and scalds on customers – especially those that take place in drive throughs. The number of hot coffee and hot tea burns and scalds have skyrocketed in recent years and believe me when I tell you that we have a disaster on our hands. Mixing drive-thru and carry-out restaurant operations with hot coffee and hot tea has proved very dangerous if not conducted with the utmost in proper training, caution, awareness, and respect.

- Chemical exposures of various types, kinds, and severities. It doesn't take a rocket scientist to figure out that toxic chemicals don't mix all that well with serving people foods and beverages that they ingest into their stomachs.

- Cuts, sprains, and strains are one thing, but severed fingers are something entirely different. Yes, the restaurant industry has lots of cuts, sprains, and strains, but we also have an astronomical number of individuals who lose fingers in a wide variety of incidents involving slicers, dicers, mixers, and dining room chairs. Yes, you read that right. Dining room chairs! I've had roughly twenty cases over the years where people have lost their fingers on the bottom of a dining room chair or table.

- Food allergy hospitalizations which account for more than 30,000 incidents annually in the United States alone, with roughly 150-200 people dying each year from allergic reactions. And oh... I should probably tell you... it's so much more than just shellfish and peanuts. It's toxic mushrooms on that pizza, oysters on that half shell, and lots more.

- Food and beverage contaminations. Some by pure unfortunate happenstance and others by intentional, hate-filled efforts by rogue employees, customers, and others to try to wreak havoc on the unsuspecting public. Some well-planned-out in a pre-meditated effort to harm, maim, and kill us and our loved ones for sport.

- Tens of thousands of separate and distinct negligent acts and liability cases that lead to multi-millions of dollars in lawsuits and insurance claims against America's restaurant and bar businesses and owners.

- Worker injuries. It is estimated that the restaurant industry accounts for more than 30% of all workplace

accidents and costs the industry billions of dollars annually.

- The restaurant industry has some of the highest employee turnover numbers of any industry and has a longstanding history of being a difficult industry within which to hire and retain new employees.

- The industry also has a very high rate of business failures and bankruptcies, with business start-up failures at the top of the charts and regularly exceeding failure rates of more than 80%.

Government organizations are well-aware of the statistics associated with the restaurant industry and the kinds of incidents that take place in restaurants each day, but rarely do they communicate them to the public, or to the restaurant industry participants themselves. Those in charge of the big restaurant chains are, or certainly should be, well-aware too.

To be fair and certain, all restaurants are not unsafe.

In fact, many are quite safe, indeed. And all restaurant owners, managers, executives, employers, and employees are not untrained, unaware, disengaged, lazy, lackadaisical, or dangerous, but, sadly, from what I see, far too many are.

It only takes one dangerous restaurant, or one dangerous restaurant owner, manager, executive, or front-line employee, and someone's life or quality of life can be damaged, destroyed, or lost forever.

The Types and Causes of Slip and Falls

So, we know the magnitude of these restaurant disasters, but let's look more specifically at what happens on the floor that causes an average of 11,000 slips and falls a day.

Slip and falls can be classified into a few basic types:

- Slip caused when there is insufficient slip resistance between a person's foot (shoe) and the walking surface (floor); this is also referred to as an insufficient coefficient of friction (COF) resulting in a slip/sliding motion throwing off one's center of gravity and balance, causing him/her to fall.

- Trips are caused when one catches his/her foot on an unexpected, raised surface (or object) in his/her pathway. This book isn't really about that, but they do classify as another kind of fall. The same goes for stumbling, which is caused when one's foot suddenly encounters an object or raised flooring surface which abruptly impedes his/her walking stride.

- Falls can also be caused by unexpected step-downs which occur with sudden changes in elevation of the flooring surface.

- Other kinds of falls are also caused by forced twisting/ rotation which occurs when one encounters an object that forces the foot or ankle to suddenly turn and can no longer reasonably support the pressure of walking.

Where protection is required, employers must select fall protection systems and procedures appropriate for the given situations, use proper implementation and installations of safety systems, supervise employees properly, and train workers in the appropriate selection, use, and maintenance of all protection systems, procedures, and equipment.

The Most Common Causes of Slip and Falls

Many different types of contaminates or obstacles can cause a slip or fall, even though offal usually is the main culprit.

According to NIOSH (National Institute of Occupation Safety and Health), there is a list of the top ten slip and fall hazards, but this book is about the single most deadly, prominent, and subtle cause of these catastrophes that beats all other restaurant floor hazards by a long shot: offal.

Nearly every slip and fall case I take comes right back to that greasy stuff on the floor that no one even seemingly and readily recognizes is there, let alone are well versed to industry standard on how best to clean it off and keep it off.

The Secret Sauce Behind the Problem - Offal: The Protein-Based Grease

As I mentioned previously, an industry recognized hazard is the protein-based grease, often referred to in the industry as "offal" or simply "grease", which is derived from the handling of, use of, storing of, and cooking of the internal meats, organs, and entrails of a butchered animal used for food products such as the meat, the liver, the kidney, and the consumable portions of beef, chicken, pork, and fish. It can also come from the greases and oils used in the cooking processes. Offal is substantially inherent to the restaurant industry and is recognized by OSHA, HACCP, the restaurant associations and many others as a slip and fall hazard.

Aside from creating a bad smell if the restaurant is not kept clean, degreased, and sanitized after the processing of any meats, it is typical for the offal-based moisture to create a slick and hazardous surface on floors and fixtures across the entire restaurant premises, both back-of-house and front-of-house, and sometimes it will even extend out the front and back doors of the premises.

The restaurant should be designed to prevent odors, discharge, splatter, and spillage of offal with the proper use of exhaust ventilation, extraction/collection systems, processing areas with raised or lipped edges, drip pans, etc. The floors should be regularly cleaned, deck-brushed, degreased, and sanitized in an industry standard manner in order to reduce and remove various protein-based greases, cooking grease, and offal on a daily, weekly, monthly, and quarterly basis using the reasonable and customary tools of the trade in order to do so.

OSHA even states that environmental conditions that increase the risk of slip and falls include poor housekeeping, improper cleaning methods and products, and inadequate or missing signage. Most of which fails to prevent the buildup of offal.

In the process of designing for the workplace, OSHA advises using adequate ventilation to avoid smoke, steam, and condensation of water and grease onto the floor.

Restaurant Slip & Falls
Mostly Preventable

So Why Do They Happen?

Employees & Management
are Ignorant (Untrainded)

Employees & Managers are
Apathetic (They Don't Care)

Employees & Managers
are Lazy

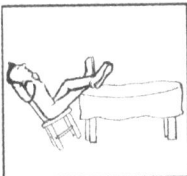

Employees & Managers are
Lackadaisical (Asleep at the Wheel)

So...

Floors Don't Get Regularly Cleaned
& Maintained Causing Grease
to Build Up

They Mostly Happen Because of Management Neglect

The 4 Biggest Slip and Fall Hazards in Restaurants and Bars

Now that you can clearly see some of the problems that are facing restaurant and bar owners, managers, executives, and decision-makers, individually and from an industry perspective as a collective whole, it's time to dig into the cause or, at the very least, the root cause of these problems.

Yes, I already pointed out the causes and types of problems regarding slip and falls, but the real hazards behind any terrible accident are the root problems in people's minds and hearts. I call them, "The 4 Biggest Hazards".

These are the four biggest hazards that are most likely to injure, harm, sicken, maim, or kill customers and employees in any restaurant, bar, food and beverage industry establishment. In this case, they are the four biggest hazards that are most likely to lead to a slip and fall incident where a customer or an employee gets injured, harmed, maimed, or killed. But they can be applied to almost any restaurant disaster we have mentioned, and beyond.

All four of them directly involve the management people of the restaurant or bar premises. These are the individual people and the collective team that has been put into a position of authority, oversight, supervision, and management of the safety, health, and security of people and premises at the specific location of the restaurant and bar. This does not necessarily mean that they work at this specific address location full-time, part-time, or anytime. It just means that they are either on the frontlines at the subject restaurant or bar location, or they have a purview of responsibility of that subject establishment in some form or fashion.

I have found after years of research that the actions or inactions of people, and most specifically anyone in charge, can be, and often is, the most dangerous element on the premises of any restaurant or group of restaurants. Simply stated, if the people in charge know, care, and act accordingly, then, typically, so do the people working for them. Conversely, if the people in charge don't know, don't care, or don't act accordingly, then, typically, the people working for them don't either.

Remember the old saying, "Crap rolls downhill?" Maybe that's just the language of my Wisconsin roots, but you know what I'm getting at. From my education, training, and experience, crap most certainly does roll downhill.

So, what are the four hazards that are most likely responsible for the huge number of incidents that injure, harm, sicken, maim, and kill restaurant and bar industry customers and employees? I'm glad you asked. They are:

#1 - Ignorance: Those in charge don't know what they are supposed to be doing, how to do it, or why it's even important.

#2 - Apathy: Those in charge don't care or don't care *enough* to do the job and take the role and responsibility that they are being paid for seriously. More often than not, they simply don't care enough about people in general, or your individual safety, health, and security at all.

#3 - Laziness: Those in charge simply don't do what they know they should be doing out of pure laziness.

#4 - Lackadaisicalness: Those in charge are asleep at the wheel and forget to do the things that made them successful and things that they used to regularly do, mostly due to boredom and lack of recent oversight and motivation. Yes. Really!

Those are the four biggest, most colossal, most dangerous hazards in any restaurant or bar. Those are the four things that are most likely to get someone – customers, employees, vendors, and others – injured, harmed, sickened, maimed, or killed in any of them across America and around the world. I know you might have been expecting something more, or something significantly different but truly it is not that complicated, and it's really not super sexy, but it is what it is.

The blame mostly gets directed at the person in charge of the restaurant and the person that they report to.

Now, for certain, there will be plenty of additional blame to spread around, but it's those two individuals (the person most in charge of the individual restaurant and bar and the individual that that person directly reports to) who are most on the hook.

You see, there will be other hazards and dangerous conditions.

There will be other operational and management train wrecks.

There will be other industry standards that are violated.

But nearly all of them end up coming back to these same four things, these four biggest hazards that are perpetuated by the person or people in charge.

The four hazards are at the same time both quite simple and highly complex. They are at the same time easy to wrap your head around and yet very difficult to comprehend. Sad, but true.

It stands to reason that…

If the boss doesn't know what is to be done, the employees surely won't either.

If the person in charge doesn't care about safety, health, and security then why would the employees?

If the owner, the general manager, the company executive, the office support person, and/or the risk manager is lazy and lax, it stands to reason that the subordinate managers and employees in the chain of command will also become lazy and lax in reasonably short order.

If the person creating and managing the standards; the individual writing and distributing the company policies and procedures; the guy or gal who created the safety rules and the operating systems has slacked off on the job and spends the majority of his or her day sitting in the office rather than running the joint, why would the employees care about much of anything?

If the guy or gal with the bigger title and better paycheck is proverbially, and sometimes even literally, falling asleep at the wheel, who in their right mind would expect the employees to be awake and do any better?

Why would they want to be engaged when the boss is not?

Why would they implement the policies, procedures, standards, and systems when he or she doesn't?

Not only does crap roll downhill, it gains speed as it goes down, but the fruit doesn't fall all that far from the tree, either (cheesy and cliché, I know, but I did say I was a Wisconsinite).

The people most responsible for the safety, health, and security of people and premises can change the trend and resolve these types of issues before something bad happens, but many times they simply don't. They sit passively by, doing nothing, and then when something bad does happen, the big red alarm goes off in their head. Sometimes that alarm is the sound of an ambulance at the front door of the restaurant. Other times that alarm is the sound of them talking to themselves saying, "I really should have trained my employees better." Or "I really should have followed up on the operation and the employees more thoroughly." From experience, I can tell you that yes, it usually is that cut and dry.

So, let's deep dive a bit into each of these hazards because each one is extremely important to these cases and the outcomes derived from them.

#1 - Ignorance - Those in Charge Don't Know

For this situation I use the word "ignorance" when referring to a lack of training and understanding. Those in charge of the restaurant or bar don't know what they are supposed to be doing or how they are to be doing it. Often the issue is that no one spent the time to teach them the "why" behind what makes it even important to begin with.

The moment you are given a title that reflects anything related to management of a restaurant or bar and the other employees that work there, you are instantaneously given the responsibility to provide management oversight for the safety, health, and security of the people and the premises, whether you like it or not.

Sure, there are other roles and responsibilities too, but it all comes down to the safety, health, and security of people and the safety, health, and security of the premises – first.

Ot at least, it should.

That means that the boss, regardless of the level of authority or compensation that they have been given, has voluntarily assumed the responsibility for the safety, health, and security of the employees, the customers, the vendors, and any other living and breathing soul that enters the premises that is under their purview of responsibility.

Simply stated, if someone in authority says, "Hey you! Will you watch the restaurant while I run this deposit to the bank?" Once that offer is accepted, that person has now just accepted the role and responsibility to provide competent person oversight for the safety, health, and security of the people and the premises. The "real boss" leaves to run the errand, and the "new boss" has just accepted and ceased responsibility.

The same can be said for shift managers, assistant managers, general managers, district managers, kitchen managers, dining room managers, and the like.

If something bad happens, where anyone gets injured, harmed, sickened, maimed, or killed in that twenty minutes, two hours, or whatever length of time they are left in charge while the "real boss" is gone and this "new boss" or

"lower-level" boss is left in charge, then the safety, health, and security training and management oversight skills, talents, and knowledge of the entire organization is placed squarely on the shoulders of the person that is left there with the new found authority – and trust me they will be placed under the bright lights and scrutinized from every imaginable angle. They will be looked at through the most powerful microscopes: the industry standards and the law.

If anyone slips, falls, and gets injured under their watch – trust me when I say this, all management-level personnel will have their safety, health, and security training and management oversight of their specific premises dissected by experts, lawyers, judges, and jurors.

If the person or persons temporarily placed in charge of the premises are doing the job, and meeting their roles and responsibilities to the standards, then no one has anything to worry about.

But if they individually or collectively are not, there are no excuses that will feed the bulldog of or stop the snowballing of the intensity of a lawsuit.

You see, in the restaurant world there *is* an "I" in "team", because if one person gets injured and we go and find out that it was because one person dropped the ball, the entire team and the entire business is going to pay for the price.

Quite honestly, it doesn't matter that the highest-ranking management person was not onsite that day.

It doesn't matter that the owner was on vacation in the Bahamas and hadn't been there in weeks.

It doesn't matter who everyone else wants to throw under the bus.

It doesn't matter that the manager is brand spanking new and hasn't received all of her training yet.

If an individual has been given authority, then they have a management role and responsibility. If they have responsibility, they better know their role, they better know their stuff, and they better be managing the stuff, the people, the premises, the systems, and the standards.

Ignorance is no excuse.

The moment a person agrees to be placed in charge, it is the responsibility of those that placed them in charge to ensure that the person in charge is competently trained, reasonably knowledgeable, reasonably aware, and prudently educated as to what needs to be done when in charge.

That includes, but is not limited to, knowing how to recognize and resolve risks and hazards during every single second while they are in charge.

It is also their own responsibility to know these things before agreeing to and accepting the role of being placed in charge.

Yes, they are responsible for themselves, their training, and those that they are being asked to watch over and protect. That takes the term, "It's all on you" to a whole new level don't you think?

I believe in my heart of hearts that in my putting forth the effort to help fix safety and security ignorance, by providing education, awareness, training, and understanding, that I might inspire restaurant owners and managers to perform significantly better in the other three biggest hazard areas of: apathy, laziness, and lackadaisicalness as well.

It stands to reason, if you know more, you will likely care more, do more, and be more aware and more engaged.

Any manager can best show their heart by focusing on prioritizing the safety, health, and security of others and thus towards showing that they care enough about the safety of others to get themselves trained, to implement and consistently execute on what they have been trained to do, and then to stay consistently and continually vigilant going forward.

Nasty incidents that change the course of a person's life usually happen in the blink of an eye. They happen sometimes literally quicker than you can snap your fingers.

An employer's role and responsibility include getting the training that they need, so that they can easily and seamlessly assess risk, recognize hazards, remove, mitigate, eliminate, or warn of the hazard, and train (or be sure that all training is getting completed) for all employees under their purview of responsibility.

This is the case regardless of whether, or not, the employees are direct reports, indirect reports, or several layers below in the chain of command. This also applies if this is even some sort of limited supervisory role.

So, now you know the number one hazard in any restaurant: ignorance. Those in charge simply don't know. They are effectively untrained.

Let's move on to number two.

#2 - Apathy - Those in Charge Don't Care

Ignorance is not knowing what the standards, systems, hazards, best practices, policies, procedures, safety rules, tools of the trade, operational policies, and risk management guidelines are.

Apathy is not caring enough about them to try to protect the safety, health, and security of people and premises, or not caring enough about the people who could be impacted if something bad happens.

More harshly still, not caring enough about the safety of man or mankind.

I see this more today than I ever have before during the course of my career.

Many people simply don't care.

As a society we have lost our love, our kindness, our concern, and our empathy for our fellow man, woman, and child.

An apathetic owner, manager, district manager, or company executive is quite possibly even more dangerous than an ignorant one. Why? Well, if they don't care, no matter what I or anyone else says or does, it won't change them much.

What makes it worse in my world is this: I can teach people what they need to know all day long, but whether they care enough or not to implement what they know is all up to them. I don't get a say in that, other than praying for them that God softens their heart at some point and helps them recognize the error of their ways and they start to care.

I just don't understand that kind of thinking.

Why on earth would anyone sign on to be a management person of some sort, in the restaurant or bar industry, the hospitality industry, by every definition, "the service of people" business, and then that person doesn't care enough about people to put forth a reasonable, customary, and prudent amount of time and effort to try to protect them as best as they possibly can?

I can certainly help improve what's rattling around in their mind, but what they feel in their heart is between them and God.

How that applies here is simply this: I want them to care for others enough so that they learn what they need to learn, so that they will try to do their absolute best to protect themselves and others – and keep people from being harmed on their watch.

I don't think that is too much to ask.

I see it regularly in deposition testimonies more often than I care to admit. I read it, and the apathetic statements jump off the page at me.

It's in those instances that it becomes quite easy for me to opine that the person giving testimony just doesn't seem to care. Usually, the jury can easily see it too. At the conclusion of those lawsuits, those management people, owners, employees, and executives who provided significant evidence and displayed behaviors that screamed out loud that they really didn't care all that much usually end up getting fleeced.

Just to be real for a moment, history shows me that management people and owners who don't really care end up costing boatloads of dollars, sometimes unfathomable amounts of money, during lawsuits and judgements.

Juries clearly don't like defendants that don't care.

They don't like bosses, managers, owners, employers, employees, vendors, and executives that don't care either. This is especially true when someone gets injured, harmed, sickened, maimed, or killed by the actions, or inactions, of a person, or people, at a restaurant or bar, that don't seem to care.

Either just before or just after these huge payouts come to bear, many times "the light turns on," and the person, or people, most responsible for the safety, health, and security of people and premises instantly begin to care.

It's usually more like this: they begin to care that they are about to lose hundreds of thousands or even millions or tens of millions of dollars. I can usually see the writing on the wall and recognize this phenomenon a bit before that moment of truth and clarity comes to light to them.

The signs, the symptoms, and the behaviors tend to reveal themselves more clearly when one is dealing with the internal angst, the worry, the stress, and the impact of the overwhelming pressures placed on them by the lawyers, the judges, the jury, their insurance carrier, and their dwindling bank account.

That, too, is what I get paid for: reading people, body language, facial expressions, and the words that come from the participants. Yes, that all can, and often times does, happen in instances where something tragic, life and death related, happens to someone in a restaurant or bar and the legal case is proceeding accordingly.

Hopefully, you will never feel the agonizing guilt like that of a manager after an employee, a customer, or a vendor has become injured, harmed, sickened, maimed, or killed on the premises under their watch.

These are gut-wrenching and heartbreaking experiences for everyone involved, me included, and I wasn't even there when any of the cases happened.

However, I do have to relive it and "bring it all back to life," if you will.

That is what a forensic expert does. He replays a past situation or incident as best as possible to try to determine what happened, who's at fault, what should have happened, and how it could have been avoided altogether in the first place.

I hope and pray that you never have to experience any of it firsthand.

The two best ways for a manager not to experience it are to be informed and to care about people. To simply care for, watch out for, and love their fellow man, woman, and child, because it's the right thing to do, and because their heart should naturally want to.

Anybody working in the restaurant industry at any level has chosen to be in the people business, where hospitality is a core building block of our industry, so they should simply deliver on that hospitality by showing that they care.

If caring just isn't their thing, they should do us all a favor and find a different way to make a living.

If you saw the negative impact these types of incidents and events have on the lives of those harmed, and the lives of their family, friends, and loved ones, you would be moved. Trust me on that one.

If it happened to someone close to you, you would be overwhelmed in too many ways to describe. Please, trust me on that one too.

It's up to management to care. If they don't, neither will those that work under them.

Let's move on to the third hazard that is most likely to harm someone.

#3 - Laziness - Those in Charge Don't Act

A manager can know all that needs to be known, care as much as his heart allows, but if he is the boss, and doesn't have the intestinal fortitude and personal motivation to get up off the office chair and actually, physically, hands-on, do something about the condition of the place, I can almost guarantee you that his or her knowledge, passion, and compassion will not resonate to the front lines and into the trenches, where restaurant and bar operations happen, and where nasty incidents happen too.

I have been doing this a very long time and people, for the most part, do not get injured, harmed, sickened, maimed, or killed in the office. It does happen, but most of the time the incident that negatively changes someone's life is in, on, or near the actual operating premises of a restaurant or bar, not at the corporate office somewhere or in the office of the restaurant itself.

But it's worth noting though the responsible parties many times reside in those offices. I say that because the person responsible many times is sitting in the office doing whatever they claim is more important at the time when the subject incident occurs.

If an owner, supervisor, or manager expects to reasonably protect customers and employees effectively, the person in charge at every level must wake up each morning and personally decide to make active choices that will make safety and security a priority and safety systems top-of-mind.

If the boss, or person with any role and responsibility pertaining to the safety, health, and security of people and premises, it is critically important that he or she takes what he or she has learned, through training and education, and shows the employees, and all of those around, that management does truly care by actually exerting the necessary effort to put those best practices, the safety rules, and those systems and standards of operation into action.

Employees will follow their management's lead, for the most

part, at nearly every level. And if that leading is crap, and crap rolls downhill, well then it gets really crappy at the bottom of the hill.

If people see her taking the extra time, putting forth the energy, and recognizing and resolving hazards to make the place as safe as it can reasonably be, they will do so as well.

Of course, alternatively, if they see her doing little to nothing, rarely leaving the office, walking past a hazard and not lifting a finger, not spending a dollar to fix a dangerous condition that is staring everyone squarely in the face, it should not be all that much of a surprise when they follow suit.

Restaurant management needs to get out of the office.

They need to get out onto the floor and into the day-to-day operations and do something. They need to make an impact. They need to drive safety as a priority and improve hazard awareness. They need to show their people that management knows, that management cares, and that management is certainly not afraid to do the work and develop the safety-first culture.

This brings us to number four. Can you even remember what it is?

I told you previously, and if you think about it a bit, you should be able to recall it from memory. It may be what you might be feeling as you watch and listen to this, or any other long training class or webinar.

Ok… times up.

I didn't want to give you too much time to mull that one over because I don't want you to lose focus and fall asleep at the wheel.

And there you have number four.

#4 - Lackadaisicalness - Those in Charge are Asleep at the Wheel

If a manager becomes lackadaisical and falls asleep at the wheel, the whole staff will begin to doze and lose focus on the day-to-day approach and implementation of safety and security awareness, systems, protocols, and standards.

Essentially, here is how it goes.

A manager and her employees are trained. She seemingly cares. She is on her feet, making things happen, and she has put a plan in motion to reduce risks and recognize and resolve hazards. It's been some time and nothing bad has happened. No one has been harmed, which is great.

Everything is seemingly going smoothly. The next thing you know, she starts to lose her focus, her passion wanes, she gets comfortable, and her attention to detail diminishes. A few days, weeks, and months pass, and for whatever reason, she has basically fallen asleep at the wheel. Complacency sets in. She starts believing that nothing bad ever happens here.

One day she forgets to fully execute on her daily operating systems. She doesn't follow-up on the staff like she once did. She begins to pencil whip everyone's checklists. She stops checking the doors, she stops following security systems and protocols, or she unintentionally revises the floor mopping procedures or stops doing the floor maintenance and care system altogether.

She forgets about the details and begins to look at only the bigger picture. Or maybe just the sales figures or profit and loss statement.

No management should do it, but all too often they do. Until one day, a waiter slips on his way to serve a table, and everything changes.

Safety and security of people and premises is all about the details.

Sure, the big picture, as it relates to the culture of safety that a manager and a team create and maintain, matters greatly, but the details of day-to-day systems, shifts, people, and standards are how that big picture comes to life. Staying forever focused on those details will allow a culture of safety to stand the test of time.

I know it's not all that fun. I get it.

But please hear me loud and clear, if management becomes lax, the team will more likely than not become lax too. If management takes a nap or a vacation as it pertains to safety and security, they will as well.

Incidents, accidents, mishaps, and injuries take no naps, are never on vacation, and are always random and happen on the spur of the moment. Therefore, safety systems and management and employee awareness and follow-up can't take a break.

Management must always be awake, aware, and vigilant. That's because customers, employees, vendors, and others get injured, harmed, sickened, maimed, and killed at all hours of the operating day, every day of the operating week, twenty-four hours a day, seven days a week, three hundred and sixty-five days a year.

You must be cognizant of this and must never lose your personal drive to protect the employees and customers that are relying on you to provide competent person oversight.

Restaurants cannot and must not waver as you strive to improve the safety and security of their premises every shift, every day, each week, all month and every month, all year long. Yes, it is that important and it does take an all-out, all hands-on deck effort.

So often when the decision-makers decide to take action, turn-over a new leaf, implement new operating systems, and engage in safety and security training, the fire will burn bright for a few days, maybe even a few weeks or several months, but they need to be aware that the fire, the flame, and the passion that drove the desire to be a better safety and risk manager can cool over time. Old habits and attitudes can come creeping back in. They can become complacent and so can members of their staff.

It is vital to fight against boredom, laziness, the lackadaisical nature that can creep back in with safety and security systems. To do that it is important to change things up, continue to learn and grow, place different people in charge of the safety programs and training, and create systems that have several different members following up and providing oversight.

So, there you have it.

The four hazards most likely to injure, harm, sicken, maim, or kill customers, employees, vendors, and others in any restaurant:

#1 – Ignorance: Those in Charge Don't Know

#2 – Apathy: Those in Charge Don't Care

#3 – Laziness: Those in Charge Don't Act

#4 – Lackadaisicalness: Those in Charge are Asleep at the Wheel

After an entire career, spanning several decades, and dealing with a potpourri of incidents, accidents, mishaps, and catastrophic events that led to a shocking number of people being injured, harmed, maimed, raped, or killed in an extraordinary number of different ways in America's restaurants and bars, I have determined that management, or lack thereof, is often to blame.

If something bad happens in a restaurant one or more of these four hazards will likely be a major contributing factor.

If you are dealing with the CEO or COO, the Vice-President or Director of Operations, a Risk Management or Human Resources leader, or some other person sitting at the corporate office with a fancy title and a decent paycheck, that has been given direct or indirect responsibilities pertaining to safety, security, risk and oversight of a restaurant or group of restaurants, everyone will want to know what roles and responsibilities that he or she bears.

People who are multi-unit managers, district managers, general managers, or, for that matter, shift supervisors, kitchen managers, team leaders, or trainers at the unit, or multi-unit levels, will have the light brightly shining on them as well.

Anyone with any roles, responsibilities, or authority, of any type or kind, will be looked at and their words and actions will be scrutinized.

I think that we can all agree that no one wants or needs any of that hassle, so restaurants are best off getting their management moving forward so that they can get trained and educated, engaged, and active, and so that they can do the same for the employees that work for and rely on them.

The key is knowing how to recognize and resolve the hazards before something bad happens. That makes sense, right?

Like I have said a thousand times before, it all starts with the training and education of the managers and then the managers sharing their training and education with all the employees.

DON'T SWEEP THE STANDARDS UNDER THE RUG

PICK THE RIGHT CLEANING PRODUCTS
10 Out of 18 Approved Products Make the Floor More Slippery!

USE MATS & CARPETS CORRECTLY
Don't Let People Track Grease or Water Through the Dining Room.

LOOK AT THE WEATHER
Be Aware of What Customers will Track in From Outside.

REMEMBER JUDGE LEARNED HAND
Assess Risks with Liability in Mind.

P & G   V.S.   B & U

©2024 RESTAURANT EXPERT WITNESS

CHAPTER 3
The Solution: Standards from OSHA and Other Governing Bodies

OSHA IS THE primary law of the land that governs occupational safety, health, and security across the United States of America and its territories. It is without a doubt one of the most important and most impactful governing bodies that protects employees, customers, vendors, contractors, and all others who enter the worksite or the premises from being injured, harmed, sickened, maimed, or killed.

I will try my best to not bore you to tears, and I will try to cut to the chase whenever I possibly can so I don't cause you to fall asleep – but this stuff is important.

This material can be quite boring, but it is critically important to slip and fall cases in restaurants nationwide.

The safety, health, and security of every person in every restaurant industry establishment, across the entire country, is riding on just how well managers and employees, at every level, comply with safety and security rules, standards, systems, and policies and procedures in restaurants during every shift, every day, every week, and every month throughout the course of the entire year.

Those working in the restaurant industry in any capacity (with any title or any level of compensation, from the front lines to the executive suite) are required to comply with these standards and best practices and those that OSHA, the governing bodies, and the restaurant industry provides and all those standards that pertain to safety, health, and security.

Bear in mind, there is a lot more to complying with industry standards and OSHA than just plastering an OSHA poster on the wall, and it is a restaurant employer's responsibility to know what that is and how to do it. In fact, OSHA requires that they operate at their own industry standards.

Like most laws, codes, rules, and standards written by lawyers, legislatures, and politicians, these industry standards and OSHA standards can appear to be much more complex than what they really are, making them and OSHA much less effective and, certainly, much less efficient at keeping people safe, healthy, and secure than was originally intended.

Fortunately, this isn't my first rodeo, and I have been dealing with this stuff for many years, so I can help you effectively and efficiently wade through the gobbledygook and get you to the stuff that you really need to know, and quickly.

I wrote a book called "Restaurant OSHA Safety and Security" that was published back in 2016 that I and my staff invested more than a thousand hours of research in, more than fourteen (14) months of writing time, and more than four-hundred thousand ($400,000) dollars of cold hard cash, out of my own pocket, to create, research, write, and distribute.

I do care for and love people, and for me, if I can help just one person avoid being injured, harmed, sickened, maimed, or killed, in one restaurant, anywhere in America, or the world, it is worth everything I have put into this.

I would rather provide the training, education, and awareness on these matters before something bad happens, rather than seeing anyone in the courtroom with me arguing against them after something bad happens.

So, now you know why I have created something that would likely cause my own forensic Restaurant Expert Witness business to have fewer customers, less sales, and make less money.

I care. I care deeply. I want to see everyone safe in restaurants and bars of their choice.

I truly believe that if together we can help prevent just one person being injured, harmed, sickened, maimed, or killed in one of America's (or the world's for that matter) restaurants or bars, then it was well worth the countless number of hours of writing and research that it took for me to complete these books and the extreme amount of effort that it took for me and my staff to get them to you.

Again, I implore you to understand this simple statement.

Restaurants and bars make up America's most dangerous industry. For an industry that so many of us love, work in, and rely on, that should cause us all some serious concern.

It's worth repeating one factor, one more time, before I let you get on with the book, because it is that important. *When those in charge don't know, I always ask myself "why"?*

Why do they not know?

Why are they uneducated and ignorant when it comes to such an important topic like reducing risks, recognizing hazards, and protecting the safety, health, and security of employees and customers in restaurants?

I once had a guy, a very successful client of mine, complain to me, "Training is so very expensive. I hate spending so much time, money, and energy training new employees, only to have them quit working for me and go to work for one of my restaurant competitors down the street (or on the other side of town) using the training that I invested in them."

I retorted back, "Look man, what's even worse than that, is you not spending the necessary time, money, and energy training your employees, and they stay employed by you untrained!"

Without training your employees, they will remain ignorant and, therefore, never be all that great of an employee.

In my world, ignorance equals danger. Untrained and uneducated equals unsafe.

It's really like this. If an owner or manager has the heart, the work ethic, the drive and determination, but doesn't know what to look for or what to do, he/she still can't create a culture of safety and still can't provide competent person oversight for the safety, health, and security of people and premises.

So...what's the solution?

To start with, restaurants need to be familiar with the governing bodies of the industry and so do those who are investigating or deposing them.

Restaurants Should Be Quite Familiar With Their Governing Bodies

These bodies provide us with a potpourri of standards, operating systems, policies, procedures, safety rules, and standards of care, but their standards are significantly different than what most people would probably think.

It is reasonable and customary for a restaurant to be operating in accordance with the laws of the land and the reasonable and customary restaurant industry standards and standards of care provided by these governing bodies.

This includes, but is not limited to, those laws, rules, standards, regulations, systems, policies, procedures, programs, protocols, guidelines, recommendations, and tools developed and implemented by various regulating bodies that govern the restaurant industry, as well as various restaurant industry leaders, restaurant industry associations, reputable restaurant industry publications and mediums, and the restaurant industry participants themselves.

These laws, rules, standards, regulations, systems, policies, procedures, programs, protocols, guidelines, recommendations, and tools – on an individual [restaurant business owner], local, state, and federal level – provide the nearly one (1) million restaurants and the nearly fifteen (15) million restaurant employees doing business across the restaurant industry throughout the United States with the restaurant industry standards, operating systems, and standards of care to provide a safe, healthy, and secure environment for customers, employees, vendors, and others who enter restaurant premises and rely on restaurant products, services, jobs, and business activity.

This includes the roles and responsibilities that all employers and all employees throughout the various restaurant industry organizations and sectors have pertaining to safety for recognizing and identifying hazards, for preventing and eliminating dangerous conditions, and much more.

To be in compliance with the restaurant industry governing bodies, standards, operating systems and standards of care, the subject establishment, its ownership, management, and employees – at every level – must take the reasonable, customary, and prudent actions to create and maintain an environment that is safe for employees, customers, vendors, and all others.

Some of these aforementioned regulating industry bodies, industry leaders, associations, and reputable publications include, but are not limited to:

- OSHA: Occupational Health & Safety Administration
- HACCP: Hazard Analysis and Critical Control Points
- DOL:U.S. Department of Labor (and State Department of Labor)
- DOH: State Department of Health
- ADA: Americans with Disabilities Act
- ANSI: American National Standards Institute
- NFSI: National Floor Safety Institute
- NSF: National Sanitation Foundation
- NRA: National Restaurant Association
- Health Departments – State, County, and Local
- Restaurant Industry Associations by State, County, National, and Local

- Industry Trade Publications
- Consultants, Authors, and Experts

The Restaurant Industry Uses a Scientific Formula of Risk for Hazard Assessment and Risk Management

I know it sometimes seems like many restaurants just operate by the seat of the owner's or manager's pants. They should be using the industry standard formula for risk management and risk assessment that has been used across the industry by risk managers for several decades.

To use this scientific formula for risk, it is important for the people in charge of safety, health, and security of people and premises at the restaurant or group of restaurants to first understand the balancing of risks in restaurants to establish a reasonable person's standard of ordinary care within restaurants.

Therefore, a formula has been established that represents the risk assessment process:

"The probability of the harm potentially caused (P) must be balanced along with the gravity of the harm which could result (G), against the burden of conforming to a new and less dangerous course of action (B), along with the utility of maintaining the same course of action as it was (U)."

This formula was developed for the scientific approach to risk assessment many years ago by Judge Learned Hand. I know what you're probably thinking, but he was a real guy, you can look it up or yourself. However, this formula or risk management process is regularly and routinely used across the restaurant industry on an everyday basis.

In shorthand, this is known as:P+G v. B+U.

In other terms, it is the process of determining the likelihood [P] that harm, and/or injury of any kind will occur from a current situation in a restaurant and then determining whether to make adjustments to eliminate or remove the situation [B] based on the severity of the harm, and/or injury [G] that may occur, opposed to leaving the situation as it is [U].

In the Restaurant Industry OSHA & HACCP Guidelines Play a Major Role

When it comes to safety, health, security, and specifically slip and fall incidents and accidents where people are injured, harmed, maimed, or killed in restaurants or bars, they must understand that prosecutors will go back to see if the people in charge at the subject restaurant operated by and understood the guidelines, safety rules, policies and procedures, standards, and recommendations of OSHA and HACCP (in various forms and fashions); and whether they were abided by.

OSHA is part of the United States Department of Labor and every restaurant doing business across America must comply with OSHA. OSHA is the primary law of the land as it pertains to workplace safety and health across the United States of America and its territories. The administrator for OSHA is the Assistant Secretary of Labor for Occupational Safety and Health. OSHA's administrator answers to the Secretary of Labor, who is a member of the cabinet of the President of the United States.

The National Restaurant Association and all state Restaurant Associations nationwide, the U.S. Department of Health and Human Services, Food and Drug Administration (FDA), The Center for Food Safety and Applied Nutrition, The Centers for Disease Control and Prevention (CDC), restaurant industry insurance carriers nationwide, restaurant industry product and service providers nationwide are all committed to OSHA, and all declare that they expect OSHA guidelines to be regularly implemented.

The restaurant industry standard – and the OSHA requirement – is that every restaurant nationwide has the "Job Safety and Health – It's the Law" OSHA Poster posted on its walls. That poster states – among other things – that, *"Employers must: comply with all applicable OSHA standards and provide required training to all workers in a language and vocabulary they can understand."*

HACCP stands for Hazard Analysis and Critical Control Points, and all restaurants must comply with HACCP guidelines.

HACCP is endorsed by the U.S. Department of Health and Human Services, Food and Drug Administration (FDA), The Center for Food Safety and Applied Nutrition, The National Restaurant Association (NRA), The Centers for Disease Control and Prevention (CDC), State and County Health Departments nationwide, and State Restaurant Associations nationwide.

HACCP is a management control system in which food safety and food facilities of all types are addressed through the analysis and control of hazards from production, procurement, and handling to manufacturing, distribution, and consumption.

What is important as it pertains to slip and falls in restaurants is that HACCP guidelines apply to the physical plant where food and beverage is produced and managed, including, but not limited to, retail establishments – which means restaurants and bars and other food and beverage industry establishments.

HACCP encourages operations to develop a customized control system for their establishment based on the following principles: (1) conduct a hazard analysis regularly through regular safety checks etc. – hazards can be physical, chemical or biological;(2) identify critical control points; (3) establish critical limits for each critical control point through monitoring requirements; (4) establish critical control point monitoring requirements; (5) establish corrective actions; (6) establish recordkeeping procedures; and, (7) establish procedures for verifying the system is working as it was intended.

HACCP guidelines and operating systems play a significant role in nearly every type of restaurant and every type of restaurant incident – not just those related to the food itself, but also those incidents that occur where an employee, customer, vendor, or other individual has been injured, harmed, maimed, or killed in any type, size, or kind of food and beverage industry facility due to a slip and fall.

OSHA Guidelines Apply to Nearly Every Restaurant "Incident" Including Those Involving Customers in Shared Spaces

OSHA safety rules, codes, guidelines, policies, and best practices play a significant role and apply to nearly every type of restaurant incident – not just those related to employees, but all incidents that occur wherein an employee, a customer, a vendor, or other individual has been injured, harmed, maimed, or killed due to a slip and fall.

The reasonable and customary restaurant industry standard is that the health and safety standards (and methods) established to protect restaurant employees are the same health and safety standards (and methods) that must be implemented in order to protect restaurant customers. This is due in large part to a mostly restaurant industry specific special circumstance that is best described as common areas or shared space. This is defined as an area that is shared by both employees and customers.

More clearly said, the floors are walked on by both employees and customers, as there are no flooring areas of the restaurant that the customers utilize that the employees do not also utilize.

The walking surfaces that the customers are exposed to in those common areas or shared spaces are the same ones that the employees are exposed to. There are no potential hazards or dangerous conditions that exist in those common flooring areas or shared spaces that do not put both the customers and the employees substantially and equally at the same level of risk of being injured, harmed, maimed, or killed.

To be crystal clear, OSHA is not only designed to protect employees but also designed to protect anyone that enters the working area where employees are working and the floors that employees are walking on.

This restaurant industry specific special circumstance (which does take place in other industries, but not to the extent that it does in ours) is the area of our industry work site which is commonly referred to as the dining room, host station, lobby, bathrooms, hallways, bar area (or more generally referred to as the front of the house) of the restaurant where both employees and customers co-mingle and use all of the same flooring surfaces.

OSHA makes several references to such shared workplace and advises industry employers to establish their own safety plans, standards, policies, and procedures that incorporate not only their employees' safety but the safety of their customers as well.

Additionally, the CDC (Centers for Disease Control and Prevention) and NIOSH (National Institute for Occupational Safety and Health) state, among other things, the following, "The laws are designed to protect private sector employees, public employees (federal, state, county, and municipal employees, including public school teachers), private and public-school students, the general public, and the environment."

A Restaurant Industry Standard Does Not Have to Be Written to Be a Standard

Although written policies, procedures, and standards are an integral and necessary part of creating a strong culture of safety (as will be addressed

later), a restaurant industry standard does not always have to be given in written form for it to exist as a reasonable and customary industry standard used by participants across the restaurant industry.

In fact, not one person or entity is the holder of the key to all the restaurant industry standards, and not one governing body has that sort of authority either.

Many restaurant industry standards have stood the test of time without being written down, often because they simply make good sense. They make people and premises safer; they reduce risk and the likelihood of someone getting injured, harmed, sickened, maimed, or killed, and they meet the requirements of certain governing bodies that the restaurant industry does, in fact, regularly look to for guidance when it comes to safety, health, and security.

There are countless examples of restaurant industry standards that make restaurants, restaurant employees, restaurant vendors, and restaurant customers safe, that are not written down anywhere and cannot be cited or referenced by a page number, a particular code, guideline, law, book, policy, or standards manual.

A perfect example is this; nowhere will you find it written that an employee is not to urinate or defecate on someone's chicken, however, employees should and do know well enough not to do so.

The same can be said for greasy floors. No matter the scenario if the employee is standing on a greasy flooring surface that is – and should be – enough to tell the employee to resolve the greasy flooring surface issue.

Therefore, certain standards can be attributed to the use of reasonable and customary common sense and prudence, which OSHA refers to many times throughout its guidelines, as does HACCP and other safety, security, and risk-related codes, guidelines, and training programs.

The General Duty Clause of OSHA is Critical to Risk Reduction and Safety Awareness for the Restaurant Industry

This General Duty Clause is many times generally cited across our industry when no other specific industry standard or specific OSHA standard, code, guideline, or recommendation applies to a particular hazard.

I won't dig into the law or the code with you too much here, because I certainly do not want to bore you to tears but the General Duty Clause of OSHA is critical to risk reduction, safety awareness, safety, health, and security compliance in the restaurant industry – no matter how big or small the restaurant business or company is and no matter the type or kind of restaurant being operated.

Why is this important to know?

Well, it is critically important to know that a safety, health, or security hazard, even if it is not specifically referenced or addressed by OSHA, may fall under the General Duty Clause of OSHA and, therefore, becomes an industry standard in the restaurant industry whether it has been specifically cited or referenced.

The General Duty Clause plays a critically important role across the restaurant industry because it is impossible for OSHA, or anyone else for that matter, to know the specifics of every single industry out there, or for anyone to think of, recollect, or conceive of every single potential hazard or dangerous condition that could possibly ever exist throughout all the different industries, let alone any one specific industry or one particular subject matter like dangerous flooring surfaces or how best to prevent them in restaurants.

This is important to note because it includes, but is not limited to, the restaurant industry. It would be impossible and absurd to expect every possible hazard, and then turn each and every one of those potential hazards into a written industry standard, an OSHA standard, and/or a restaurant site specific standard. This would take a herculean effort that I can't even fathom to be possible and would certainly not be reasonable.

Here is basically what OSHA's General Duty Clause (GDC) says: "*SEC. 5. Duties: 29 USC 654, (a) Each employer -- (1) shall furnish to each of his employees, employment and a place of employment which are free from recognized hazards that are causing or are likely to cause death or serious physical harm to his employees; (2) shall comply with occupational safety and health standards promulgated under this Act. (b) Each employee shall comply with occupational safety and health standards and all rules, regulations, and orders issued pursuant to this Act which are applicable to his own actions and conduct."*(osha.gov)

It is important to understand that restaurant industry employers, managers, owners, and executives who are responsible for the safety, health, and security of people and premises must be trained, must always be on the lookout for hazards and dangerous conditions, and must recognize that their responsibilities reach far beyond just the hazards that have been specifically identified and provided by OSHA, HACCP, ADA, and others – even those previously identified by restaurant industry trade organizations or experts.

Reasonably, the owners, operators, executives, and managers – which is easier to identify by 'those in charge' – must seek to use their own training, education, and experience to identify, remove, eliminate, resolve, and/or warn of dangerous conditions and hazards reasonably and customarily. This must be done regularly, consistently, and continually. It must be the case even if those hazards and dangerous conditions have not been previously identified by them or others.

Simply stated, just because a particular hazard or dangerous condition is not specifically referenced in an OSHA Standard or has not been previously identified by others across the industry does not mean that an employer is not required to look to find new hazards and isn't responsible to implement safety measures and safety rules to remove a hazard or a dangerous condition in which someone – anyone - could reasonably become injured, harmed, sickened, maimed, or killed by.

In fact, it is quite to the contrary. If a hazard or dangerous condition exists, it is a restaurant industry standard that the hazard or dangerous condition must be blocked off, eliminated, reduced, removed, or warned of by restaurant management and employees immediately upon being noticed, in order to reasonably and customarily attempt to keep premises safe and people free from harm.

A Standard in Other Industries Becomes a Standard for Restaurants

When a recognized hazard or dangerous condition from another industry becomes apparent within the restaurant industry, or within an industry workplace, the OSHA standard and industry standards pertaining to that hazard or dangerous condition would reasonably and customarily apply to the restaurant industry or that restaurant industry specific workplace as well.

All restaurants must abide by all recognized restaurant industry standards regardless of whether they are specifically referenced by OSHA or recognized by any other industry.

If a condition is considered to be dangerous or hazardous in any industry other than the General Industry as cited by OSHA (such as on a farm or a construction site, for example) and the same or a similar type of dangerous or hazardous condition exists in a restaurant, but OSHA does not speak directly to that specific condition as it relates to restaurants in its standards for General Industry. Then, the OSHA standard or industry standards that apply to that dangerous or hazardous condition for the other industry would also reasonably and customarily apply to the restaurant, as any unsafe condition must be addressed regardless of the industry in which it exists.

Is it Federal OSHA or State OSHA Guidelines that Must be Followed?

Federal OSHA guidelines state that even in instances where an individual state has its own State OSHA regulations, the most stringent safety guidelines of either the State or the Federal OSHA guidelines must apply.

Meaning that in every instance, the Federal OSHA guidelines become, at the very least, the bare minimum guideline that must be met – because State Plans must set workplace safety and health standards that are at least as effective and stringent as the Federal OSHA standards. Many State Plans adopt standards identical to Federal OSHA.

Employee and Employer Safety Responsibilities

The reasonable and customary restaurant industry standard is that all employees have a responsibility for creating and maintaining a safe environment and must be trained to do so.

Likewise, the reasonable and customary restaurant industry standard is that the employer has a responsibility for creating and maintaining a safe environment and must be trained to do so. The employee and/or manager on behalf of the employer must also train his/her employees to do so. This requirement is crystal clear on every wall poster provided by OSHA to every restaurant doing business anywhere across the United States (See OSHA Wall Poster).

Restaurant Managers Must Focus on Employee Training

Employee training programs should be designed to ensure that all employees understand and are aware of the hazards to which they may be exposed and the proper methods for avoiding such hazards.

Supervisors should be trained to understand the key role they play in job site safety and to enable them to carry out their safety and health responsibilities effectively.

One of the recommendations by the United States Department

of Labor and OSHA is that all employees at the restaurant are trained to recognize hazards and to report any hazard they find to the appropriate person so that the hazard can be corrected as soon as possible. In addition to taking the immediate action of reporting a hazard, they must provide interim protection, if necessary – including stopping the work which is causing the hazard.

The employer must instruct each employee in the recognition and avoidance of unsafe conditions, and in the regulations applicable to his or her work environment to control or eliminate any hazards or other exposure to illness or injury immediately upon recognition.

The restaurant decision makers have a duty that is owed to each employee. In fact, the employer must train every employee in the manner required by the industry standard, and the standards provided by the governing body, and each failure to train an employee may be considered a separate violation.

Training must be a reasonable and customary process which is ongoing and continual for each individual employee. Ongoing training must include written, verbal, video, formal, informal, and hands-on training that is in direct alignment with the written policies, procedures, and practices of the restaurant industry, the overall restaurant organization, and the specific restaurant establishment to be within industry standard and in regulatory compliance.

According to OSHA, training is an essential component of an effective safety and health program. Training of all staff members is the most important job of restaurant managers and owners.

Training Must Be provided in a Language that the Employee Understands

The reasonable and customary restaurant industry standard is to provide employee training in a language that each employee understands. Not only is this industry standard and simple common sense, but OSHA also specifically requires employers to present information in a manner and language that their employees can understand.

If employers customarily need to communicate work instructions or other workplace information to employees in a language other than English, they will also need to provide safety and health training to employees in the same manner. Similarly, if the employee's vocabulary is limited, the training must account for that limitation.

By the same token, if employees are not literate, telling them to read training materials will not satisfy the employer's training obligation. This is clearly stated in the OSHA Wall Poster that is provided to every restaurant doing business anywhere in the United States.

Restaurants Must Have the OSHA Wall Poster Visibly Present

It is a law that all restaurant industry employers must post the OSHA Wall Poster or the state plan equivalent in a prominent location somewhere in the restaurant. They are usually posted either in the kitchen area of the restaurant or in the office that all employees can easily access and see. The Wall Poster comes in several different languages, and they are all available free of charge.

The OSHA Wall Poster must be made available in the language that each employee understands. This is clearly stated in the OSHA Wall Poster that is provided to every restaurant doing business anywhere in the United States.

Slip and Falls: Hazards Recognized by Several Regulating Bodies Including OSHA and National Institute for Occupational Safety & Health (NIOSH)

Specific slip and fall injuries are recognized by these regulating bodies as follows: sprains, strains, bruises, and contusions from slip and falls.

It is estimated that more than three million food service employees and more than one million restaurant industry guests are injured annually because of restaurant slips, trips, and falls according to the National Floor Safety Institute (NFSI).

According to the National Restaurant Association, slips and falls are the greatest source of general liability insurance claims within the restaurant industry.

Further evidence of this highly recognized danger is stated by OSHA as follows: *Slips, trips, and falls from these surfaces constitute the majority of general industry accidents.*

These same aforementioned regulating bodies have noted other recognized restaurant industry hazards which include, but are not limited to, cuts and lacerations from knives and other tools, heat burns from hot oil, steam, hot water and hot surfaces, bending, lifting, and pushing injuries, workplace violence and elevated homicide risks, and exposure to chemicals, biological materials, and smoke. But no other incident has the sheer number like that of slip and fall incidents.

These are well-publicized hazards and should not come as a surprise to anyone that is responsible for the management of people and premises in the restaurant industry. The restaurant industry does have a significant number of recognized hazards and is considered by the governing bodies to be a potentially dangerous environment for employees and customers alike. For anyone to think otherwise is neither reasonable nor prudent.

I would say that this is especially true in restaurants where management and owners do not create and maintain a culture of safety. In restaurants such as these, incidents where customers, employees, and others get injured, harmed, sickened, maimed, and/or killed tend to occur on a more frequent basis or, at the very least, the likelihood of these types of events occurring is higher.

The U.S. Justice Department and Department of Labor have set minimum safety guidelines for walkway safety that are enforced under OSHA and ADA (Americans with Disabilities Act). In 2001, the American National Standards Institute (ANSI) published a "Standard for the Provision of Slip Resistance on Walking/Working Surfaces" which describes methods for testing walkway surfaces as well as enhancing the safety of walkway materials.

In June of 2006, the NFSI (The National Floor Safety Institute) was recognized by ANSI as an Accredited Standards Developer. NFSI provides a Self-Inspection Checklist regarding Walking and Working Surface Requirements, which includes, among other things:

- *Flooring, Stairs, and Walkways:* Inspect walkway surfaces for hazards including holes, chips, cracks, elevations ...; Stairways and changes in interior elevations should be well lighted and free of obstacles. Floors, stairs, and walkways should be kept clean and dry (free from spillage); free of protrusions, obstacles and debris; floor holes or openings (such as floor drains) should be guarded by a cover, guardrail or equivalent on all sides (except at entrance to stairways); floor mats and non-slip materials should be provided where necessary (especially entrance doors in inclement weather); and, they should be level (no sudden or hidden change in elevation) and safe to transverse (walk on) without fear of slip or falls (any changes in elevation should be properly illuminated).

- *Hazard Identification:* Post caution signs for all potentially hazardous walkways; mark all physical hazards, including inclines, drop-offs, and temporary walkways ...

- *Inspections:* Inspect walkways regularly (minimum of once per hour); it is recommended that walkway surfaces be audited on a regular basis to identify and eliminate potential slip hazards.

- *Employee Training:* Uniformly train employees about established safety procedures, stressing that safety is everyone's job; provide all employees with a consistent level of product usage training; post written slip and fall prevention and accident handling policies on employee bulletin boards; keep a training log for each employee to sign

that acknowledges they were trained on the company's comprehensive slip and fall prevention strategy.

These strategies, policies, and industry standards seem simple, I know, but they can be the difference between a restaurant's success and failure, or a person's life or death.

BEEF, CHICKEN, PORK, AND FRIED FOODS CREATE GREASE
HERE IS HOW YOU GET IT OFF THE FLOORS

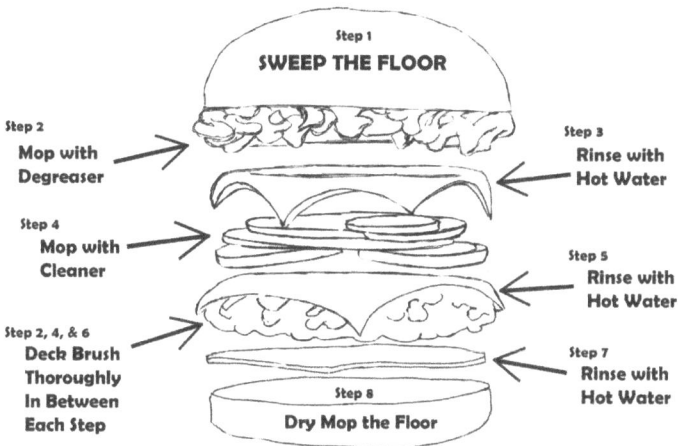

Step 1
SWEEP THE FLOOR

Step 2
Mop with
Degreaser

Step 3
Rinse with
Hot Water

Step 4
Mop with
Cleaner

Step 5
Rinse with
Hot Water

Step 2, 4, & 6
Deck Brush
Thoroughly
In Between
Each Step

Step 7
Rinse with
Hot Water

Step 8
Dry Mop the Floor

FOLLOW THESE CRITICAL STEPS SO THAT YOU DON'T GET SANDWICHED WITH A LAWSUIT

©2024 **RESTAURANT EXPERT WITNESS**

CHAPTER 4
The Solution: The Reasonable and Customary Industry Standards & Other Crucial Things You Need to Know

E*VEN THOUGH CERTAIN standards are listed in OSHA and other governing bodies, there are some essential practices every restaurant should be following to comply with them and there are reasonable and customary standards that come with working in the industry, written and unwritten.*

That starts with each restaurant's general culture of safety. If you are going to win your case against a negligent restaurant, you need to understand what the culture was like that caused such a terrible accident for your client.

The Worst Offenders Don't Know the Essentials to Creating a Culture of Safety

As I already told you, the four biggest hazards in any restaurant or bar where something bad has happened are fairly easy for me as a forensic testifying expert in the restaurant industry to recognize and opine about.

To recap, they are:

#1. Ignorance – Those in charge of the restaurant really don't know what it is that they are supposed to be doing. They have not been trained.

#2. Apathy – Those in charge of the restaurant really don't care all that much about the safety, health, and security of people and premises.

#3. Laziness – Those in charge of the restaurant don't do the job that they are supposed to be doing, that they have been trained to do, and that they reasonably know, or should have known to do.

#4. Lackadaisicalness – Those in charge of the restaurant have fallen asleep at the wheel and therefore their standards are low, their operational execution and risk management performance is poor, and their awareness of the risks and the bad things that could happen is nearly non-existent.

The solution is quite straight forward.

Those in charge of the restaurant need to take the necessary steps to create and maintain a culture where safety, health, and security for both employees and customers is a priority. We call this a "Culture of Safety."

In fact, I believe that the absolute best way for management to show employees, customers, vendors, community, and even the family, friends and loved ones of those who work for them, dine with them, and rely on them, that he/she as an individual in charge of the restaurant or group of restaurants truly cares about them and their loved ones is to first and foremost care about their individual and collective safety, health, and security.

And the best way to do that? Create and maintain a culture of safety at the front-line unit level on every shift, and on an everyday basis.

So, here I am going to give you the insider's secret on just how to do that and the insider's secret on the absolute best way to attack a lawsuit against any restaurant owner, operator, or manager who is not doing that.

The first thing to note is what I've already said: A culture of safety must be created and maintained by those in charge (restaurant owners, operators, managers, etc.) by taking steps to create well-planned and well-written policies, procedures, systems, and practices.

These written policies, procedures, systems, and practices must then be consistently implemented and trained and must be used by all employees throughout the organization (at every level), thereby creating shared understandings, values, and beliefs among all employers and employees of the restaurant and the restaurant company, making safety, health, and security top-of-mind for everyone.

A culture is a general attitude and atmosphere created by those beliefs which eventually guide and shape the behaviors of every individual within the establishment and throughout the entire organization. The reasonable and customary restaurant industry standard of care is to create and maintain an environment of basic policies, procedures, operating systems, safety, health, and security protocols, and standards in written form that allow the management of the restaurant or a group of restaurants to create and maintain a safety-first mentality among all of the employees, commonly known throughout the restaurant industry as a culture of safety.

For a culture of safety to exist, the entire organization (all employers and all employees) must commit to safety, health, and security as being an integral part of the day-to-day restaurant operations. Everyone involved must operate with a reasonable and customary level of caution to ensure that prudence, as it pertains to safety, health, and security, is regularly and consistently exercised.

How will Creating a Culture of Safety Help?

A positive culture of safety, health, and security provides a big boost in employee morale while simultaneously improving productivity and decreasing workplace injuries, illnesses, and death to workers and customers alike.

In turn, this decrease in workplace incidents and customer

and employee injuries also lowers insurance premiums and operating expenses for any restaurant establishment.

Research shows that a strong culture of safety, above anything else, has the single greatest impact on accident reduction in the workplace. For no other reason than this, it should be the number one priority for all restaurant owners, managers, executives, decision-makers, and employers.

The Key Traits of a Strong Culture of Safety

From my forty-five plus years of hands-on experience working in the trenches of restaurants and bars across the country and around the world, I have come to realize that restaurants and bars that have a strong culture of safety, health, and security most commonly exhibit the same similar traits and practices.

Conversely, those that have weak cultures, or could even be described as unsafe cultures, also commonly exhibit the same similar and like traits to each other.

I call these little gems The Culture of Safety Essentials. We'll go over them in more detail in a minute. They are:

- Well written policies, procedures, systems, standards, and protocols that are easy to understand and are focused on expressing the things that the management holds for beliefs and deem as important.
- Shared management and employee attitudes, values, missions, objectives, and beliefs towards placing

safety, health, and security for all as priorities over sales and profits.

- Safety posters, warning signs, tools of the trade, and equipment.
- Management and supervisor priorities, responsibilities, and accountability.
- Employee motivation and involvement.
- Employee training in a language and style that every employee can individually understand.
- Continual and ongoing training for every employee during the entire length of their employment, from their first day of employment through their last day of employment.
- Regularly scheduled safety meetings and employee safety, health, and security meeting notes.
- Communications and bulletins providing safety, health, and security and hazard communications information to all employees in various forms.
- Complete, thorough, and timely incident reports after an incident occurs.
- Incident investigations on all incidents regardless of size or severity of the injury and including close calls – incidents that almost happened.
- Immediate action to correct unsafe behaviors and conditions.
- Employees who are provided with the necessary tools to safely do their assigned jobs.

- Regular site safety, health, and security audits and hazard assessments.
- An open-door policy so that employees at every level can voice their concerns and point out what they see as hazards and dangerous conditions.
- Management and ownership talk about safety, health, and security on a regular basis.

An environment where all employees have a reasonable degree of caution and prudence as it pertains to safety, health, and security in order to recognize, eliminate, mitigate, and warn of hazards and dangerous conditions that may exist anywhere on the restaurant premises and anywhere the restaurant's operations and/or business is taking place.

For a true culture of safety to exist, it is reasonable and customary to create and maintain an environment where everyone feels responsible for safety, health, and security every day.

Management and employees at every level must be vigilant about identifying, recognizing, mitigating, and removing hazards and unsafe conditions, as well as recognizing behaviors by employees, customers, and vendors that create or are likely to create a hazardous or dangerous condition in the future.

The Many Aspects of Management Support

If employees of any establishment are expected to succeed, they are only going to do so if following the leadership of management that is both supportive and clear in direction and expectations.

Restaurant management must support their staff by:

- Defining safety, health, and security responsibilities for all employees at every level.
- Forming a safety committee and appointing a safety director.
- Establishing safety, health, and security goals and measuring safety, health, and security-related activities (continually measure performance, communicate results, and celebrate successes).
- Creating incentives and disciplinary systems when needed (reward employees for doing the right things and encourage participation).
- Holding managers and supervisors, as well as employees, accountable for any unsafe or unhealthy behaviors and actions (safety is everyone's job).
- Setting a proper positive example for others to follow.
- Allowing for employee suggestions, concerns, and problems without fear of punishment or retribution.
- Creating reporting and investigation systems.

- Providing continual and ongoing training, support, feedback, and reinforcement.

Let's go over these essentials for a culture of safety in more specific detail.

The 16 Essentials for a Culture of Safety

There are sixteen (16) management essentials that must be in place to create and maintain a culture of safety in any restaurant or group of restaurants. If some of these are missing, it's likely not going to be all that good for the restaurant's case.

They consist of the following:

#1. Understand the Significance of this Industry:

Every manager should be reasonably aware that the restaurant industry employs roughly 11% of the entire US workforce and 50% of all Americans have at some point in their lives worked in the restaurant industry.

This, along with the fact that nearly everyone in America (from the very young to the very old among us) regularly frequent restaurants – and nearly half of all Americans cite a restaurant job as their very first – makes it very easy to understand just how personal and critically important restaurants are to us all.

These are not insignificant factors. They should regularly be discussed among all restaurant employees to bring focus not only to the role that restaurants play in American culture, but the roles that they themselves, as restaurant employees, play as well. This knowledge helps to instill significance in restaurant workers for the jobs that they are performing and the contributions that they are making, regardless of how long they remain employed in the industry.

#2. Written Policies and Procedures:

Every manager should take charge of his/her own well-planned written policies, procedures, operating systems, and 'what-if' scenarios (considerations for the possible effects and outcomes of expected and/or unusual and unexpected behaviors—whether the restaurant company that employs the workers has done this for them or not).

These written policies and procedures are the foundation of the entire safety, health, and security program for the restaurant operation of which management are in charge. If the company has already done this, then great. Chances are they have given a good start and possibly even a great start. But it is management's job to thoroughly review what they have been provided and not be afraid of adding more detail or putting some real "teeth" into areas where it is necessary to do so to ensure that the employees understand just how important this information is and what steps management is willing to take to ensure that they comply.

#3. Management Oversight:

Every manager who supervises someone is responsible for the safety, health, and security of people and premises.

This is true regardless of title and compensation, and regardless of the span of control and authority or the number of locations, as the manager is required and expected to be a competent person as defined by the governing bodies and industry.

#4. Getting Everybody's Arrows Aligned:

Every manager must understand that getting everyone on the same page regarding safety, health, and security is the key to safety in any restaurant or group of restaurants.

Every manager and employee should understand the specific policies, procedures, standards, and operating systems that are to be implemented to ensure compliance and operational execution with risk management in mind. Once everybody's "arrows are aligned," it is much easier to get momentum behind a new or an existing safety system.

#5. Site Analysis of the Entire Premises and All Employees:

Every manager should take personal responsibility for the entire premises (inside and out) and every nook and cranny under his/her purview (scope of responsibility) as well as the safety, health, and security of all people on and/or entering the premises.

The entire premises should be assessed and analyzed periodically and on a regular basis by management personally and by multiple layers of management and other employees so as to always have a fresh set of eyes looking at the entire facility, operation, building, furniture, fixtures, standards, and equipment. Everyone's roles and responsibilities as they pertain to safety, health, and security should be clearly spelled out, on paper. If a multi-unit manager oversees multiple locations, then that simply means that that individual has multiple premises to analyze and assess personally, in addition to documenting the efforts that they have made to do so.

#6. Continual and Ongoing Training:

Every manager should take personal responsibility for the continual and ongoing training of every employee at every level of the organization within his/her purview of responsibility.

This includes employees from the front lines to the executive suite and every position in between (dependent upon what level of authority any particular title implies, and which employees report to which management person either directly or indirectly).

Training must include continual and ongoing safety, health, and security training from the moment of each employee's initial orientation to the absolute last minute of work on the final day of employment. It does not mean that management has to do it all physically themselves (one can delegate - after all, that's one of the perks of being management), but it does mean that management must follow up to ensure that it is getting done and getting completed to industry standards and expectations.

#7. Safety Meetings:

Every manager must be involved in the restaurant establishment's safety meetings. These meetings should happen on a daily, weekly, monthly, quarterly, and annual basis.

Traditionally, daily safety meetings last only a few minutes before and after each shift. It is customary to pull everyone together into a huddle for a quick safety, health, and security review, as well as a brief pre-shift sales-building and customer satisfaction rally.

These short pre-shift meetings can have a huge impact on the overall performance and culture of any restaurant and can make all the difference between day-to-day excellence and day-to-day mediocrity, complete trainwrecks, and death traps.

Monthly, quarterly, and annual safety meetings should be conducted with a written agenda and accompanied by a sign-in sheet for all those in attendance. A memo summarizing each safety meeting discussion should be sent out to all of those who are not able to be in attendance to ensure that the message of safety, health, and security is communicated to everyone on the team.

#8. Listening to the Employees:

Every manager should fully understand that if one truly wants to know what's going on in a restaurant or what's going on in the day-to-day operations associated with that restaurant, then one should simply start by asking the employees. They will cough up what they know nearly every time.

Management should seek out their ideas and input and ask them for suggestions. They will share. After all, who wants to think that their opinions aren't of value?

The more a manager asks them, the more likely they will tell them what they need to hear, and the more likely they will begin to care about the people, the business, the restaurant, the restaurant industry, and the safety, health, and security of everyone who comes into the restaurant where they work. That's also why the employee testimonials usually hurt a restaurant's case when defending themselves in a lawsuit. A manager can pretend all day that the employees care and know what to do, but the employees actually working in the restaurant will tell a lawyer what the culture and performance at the subject location was and is really like.

#9. Turning 180 Degrees When Needed:

Every manager most certainly understands that there are times when things can get slightly off track. It happens to everyone and at every restaurant at one time or another. Hopefully, during this time, nothing bad will happen as a result, but if and when less than industry standard actions should begin to happen, it is the manager's job to recognize it and get everyone back on track as quickly as possible.

Confident decision-making and quick action are necessary for these types of situations to get the entire shift, team, and organization back in line and in compliance, especially as it pertains to safety,

health, and security. That is what management is all about, after all. So yesterday may not have been as good as a manager or employee would have liked it to be, but today is a new day, and there is no better time than the present to do a 180-degree turn and get everyone back on track.

#10. Going By the Books:

Every manager must understand and comply with OSHA, HACCP, FDA, EEOC, ADA, and the local, state, and federal governments, and the laws of the land.

There are also many general industry standards and regulations that managers are expected to abide by, comply with, and understand.

The same can be said for restaurant industry standards and those standards that are specific to a particular place of business. Knowing the books and going by the books will help keep managers off the hook, especially when or if something bad happens.

#11. Self-Education and Training:

Management should not simply rely on the occasional training provided by a supervisor to carry out their job effectively. They are best advised to take the lead in their own training and development process.

Every manager must understand that to be successful in the

restaurant industry, it is imperative to go above and beyond the call of duty and to seek out, source, and secure the reasonable and customary training, education, knowledge, and skills necessary to prudently, professionally, and safely operate a restaurant (or group of restaurants), and to ensure that the restaurants under one's purview of responsibility are safe, healthy, secure, and in compliance.

The same is true about profitability. Every manager should know what it takes to make a restaurant profitable. If someone doesn't understand how to make the business profitable then that person should not be a manager.

#12. Conduct Incident Reports and Incident Investigations:

Every manager must understand that it is their responsibility, if and when something does happen where someone becomes injured, harmed, sickened, maimed, or killed (or after any near misses), to conduct and complete a timely incident report.

Management must also conduct a thorough and timely incident investigation to prudently and responsibly collect the necessary information about what transpired, who was involved, who witnessed the events, and what caused the incident to occur in the first place.

These reports and investigations are critical in putting forth the best effort to prevent the same types of events from reoccurring in the future. What's the old saying? "A pound of prevention is better than a multimillion-dollar damages claim?" Well, something like that.

#13. Communicate, Discuss, Log, and Disseminate:

Every manager must understand that one of the most important aspects of improving safety, health, and security in any restaurant is to improve and enhance communication between management and the employees, especially as it pertains to safety, health, and security.

Restaurants need to open the lines of communication and discuss a wide variety of topics about these subject matters with every employee. They should keep good logbooks regarding incidents, systems, training, and so much more. When one has a new policy, procedure, or system, be sure to clearly disseminate the new information to everyone under their purview.

#14. Use Security Cams and Safety Tools:

Every manager must know how to work all safety tools, systems, security cameras, safe codes, back door alarms, security lights, panic buttons, and they must be prepared to do so at any time. The time to learn these things is not during an emergency.

Security cameras are great tools for reducing theft in any

restaurant, but they are also great tools for improving safety, health, and security awareness and for monitoring day-to-day operational performance and risk management. If something bad does happen, one of the first places management should check is the security/surveillance cameras to review what the actual video evidence provides.

They need to be sure that everyone knows how to preserve the video evidence, as well as the operational performance evidence, which can be observed by watching video. They will most likely need it later. If management doesn't know if the security cameras work or has never gone back to check them, that's a bad sign.

#15. Follow-up and Micro-Manage:

Every manager must have significant follow-up skills and be willing and able to sometimes micromanage employees to get the job done correctly.

A good manager understands that standards are standards and sometimes, they have to take the bull by the horns to get things done. This may require empowering fewer people and micromanaging anyone and everyone who requires it, most especially as it pertains to critical roles and responsibilities regarding safety, health, and security.

It's not always fun, but there are times when a heaping helping of management follow-up and oversight is the most effective method to improve performance in any restaurant.

#16. Make Money:

Every manager must understand and accept the simple concept that restaurants are meant to be in business to make money.

It doesn't take long to figure out that the restaurant owners and managers that are making considerable profits are traditionally the same restaurant owners and managers that are willing to put the most time, money, and effort towards safety, health, and security compliance, hazard awareness, and employee training.

Conversely those restaurant owners and managers that are struggling to make ends meet or, worse yet, losing their shirts are often not all that interested or focused on safety and training.

Of course, sometimes restaurant owners and managers are just profit machines and sales monkeys and their entire focus and culture are based on more sales and more profits and safety is simply not a priority.

I often tell crews in restaurants all over the country to "make money, be safe, and make more money." It's our simple way of saying that being in the restaurant business is about both making a profit and keeping people safe. After all, that's what all business endeavors should be about. But it is also imperative for everyone to know for any restaurant to remain in business for very long, the entire team must be laser-focused on the safety, health, and security of everyone who enters the premises, employees, customers, and vendors alike *first* with profits being second. This line of thinking is what affords us the opportunity and the privilege of staying in business and, hopefully, making even more money.

OSHA states, "*Any process that brings all levels within the organization together to work on a common goal that everyone holds in high value will strengthen the organizational culture.*"

They are, of course, referring to creating a strong culture of safety and health. A federal government agency such as OSHA believes in the power of organizational culture. Doing anything to create or maintain an environment or culture to the contrary is ill-advised, imprudent, and most likely to be considered as a case of management neglect (and will probably cost a restaurant big time later).

A restaurant company with a strong culture of safety will more likely than not experience fewer unsafe and risky behaviors from its employees and in turn will most likely experience a lower accident and incident rate, lower employee turnover and absenteeism, lower out-of-pocket expenses, and higher productivity. No matter how you slice it, that's always good for the bottom line of any restaurant!

I believe it really is as cut and dry as this. By putting forth the time, effort, and focus to create and maintain a culture of safety in a restaurant or bar, it is more likely that it will end up creating an environment that has a much stronger pulse and a much more cohesive and connected group of people working together. They will create an environment that will have a much higher propensity for eliminating the four biggest hazards of ignorance, apathy, laziness, and lackadaisical managers and employees and it will show everyone coming into the establishment that the restaurant has a team of managers and employees who care more about them than they do sales, food cost, labor cost, and profits. Management must care about customer and employee safety, health, and security *first*.

As the person in charge, he or she has to walk the talk, take actual charge, and be safe.

For those that still need more convincing, I hope and pray that they never find out just how much time, money, and energy a massive lawsuit or insurance claim against them and their restaurant or bar business will cost them after someone gets injured, harmed, sickened, maimed, or killed on their watch. It's not pretty. These are gut-wrenching and heartbreaking experiences for everyone involved.

When something bad happens at a restaurant or bar, my job is to find the facts and evidence and provide an unbiased opinion to the court, with a scientific methodology that will withstand scrutiny, so that the courts can hold those responsible, accountable for their actions or lack thereof.

The Antidotes to the 4 Biggest Slip and Fall Hazards

If someone works in the restaurant business, I would love to see them regularly asking themselves these questions as the antidotes to the four biggest hazards of ignorance, apathy, laziness, and lackadaisicalness:

#1: Am I reasonably and acceptably trained? Do I have the safety and security knowledge that is expected of me as a restaurant owner, manager, multi-unit manager, executive, employer, employee, or vendor, with the role and responsibility of reducing risks and protecting people and premises as it pertains to safety and security and more specifically as it pertains to slip and falls?

#2: Do I care about the safety and security of my employees and my customers? Do I wake up each morning and actually take care of my business by doing the things that I know I should be doing to protect the people working at and coming into the business? Am I taking charge and responsibility to reasonably ensure that the premises are safe and secure for everyone under my purview of responsibility and more specifically for this subject matter within this book – as it pertains to slip and falls?

#3: Am I working hard and putting forth the necessary effort to stay on top of my game by making sure that the place is safe and that my employees are safety-aware and fully engaged, more specifically as it pertains to slip and falls?

And finally, #4: Have I fallen asleep at the wheel? Or am I focused, diligent, consistently engaged, and aware, more specifically as it pertains to slips and falls on the premises that I am responsible for?

If you are dealing with a restaurant industry employer, employee, risk manager, manager, or executive I hope and pray that the statistics that I shared with you earlier are not new to them, and if they are that it opened up their eyes enough to help them care, and I hope and pray that they are sufficiently as concerned as I am about the dangerous conditions present in America's restaurants.

Quite honestly, if they did not shake, shock, and move you a good bit, I have no idea what will.

I'm not sure what else I could possibly say or do to emotionally move someone in the right direction, and, if a restaurant worker is still not convinced of the importance of a culture of safety, he/she would be best advised to reconsider his/her career choices. Maybe the hospitality industry, the people business, just isn't a good fit for that person.

If that is the issue, I feel bad for those employees, customers, and others that are clearly in harm's way because one or a few people don't have much of a pulse and lack the "let's get it done" kind-of-gene that used to be so engrained in the restaurant and bar industry and, for that matter, our entire social fabric.

It's up to every manager and supervisor to find that within themselves, to wake up each day and decide to do whatever they've got to do so that as much as it's up to them, they ensure everybody under their watch goes home safely at night.

The manager of a restaurant – let me rephrase – *any* manager at *any* restaurant, has the power and the ability to be the most dangerous hazard and most overwhelming factor present that leads to the place being unsafe simply by personally choosing to ignore and/or neglect his/her roles and responsibilities as it pertains to safety and security.

That same manager, owner, executive, or decision-maker can also be the greatest, most positive contributing factor to safety and security for all. It's completely up to each person to decide which one he/she is going to be.

So, what else does that look like for a manager, owner, or supervisor according to the industry standards?

Continual Training from the First Day of Employment to the Last day of Employment

The reasonable and customary restaurant industry standard is to provide every employee with continual and ongoing safety, health, and security training from the time they begin employment with the restaurant until their time of termination of employment from the restaurant.

Continual and ongoing training in the restaurant industry traditionally includes a varied mixture of written, verbal, hands-on, and video training that is in direct alignment with the written policies, procedures, and practices of the restaurant industry, the written policies, procedures, and practices of the specific restaurant organization, and the written policies, procedures, and practices of the specific restaurant establishment that the employee is working at to be within restaurant industry standard and regulatory compliance.

Training helps identify the safety and health responsibilities of both management and employees at the restaurant site. Training is often most effective when incorporated into other education or performance requirements and job practices pertaining to the restaurant industry or the specific restaurant where the employee is employed. The complexity of training depends on the size and complexity of the restaurant worksite, brand, or company, as well as the specific characteristics of the hazards and potential hazards at the restaurant itself.

Make no mistake about it – restaurants and restaurant operations are highly complex, and the hazards and potential hazards are many.

Many OSHA standards, which have prevented countless workplace tragedies, include explicit safety, health, and security training requirements to ensure that workers have the required skills and knowledge to safely do their work.

Of note, these requirements reflect the universal and fundamental belief of our industry – and of OSHA – that training is an essential part of every employer's safety, health, and security program for protecting workers and customers from various types and kinds of slip and fall injuries and from all manner of slip and fall hazards.

Also of particular note is research that has discovered and concluded that those who are new on the job have a much higher rate of injuries and illnesses than more experienced workers unless those long tenured workers have a history of not being provided training and management follow-up oversight; in which case tenured workers can be much more dangerous. The same can be said for customer slip and fall injuries where the workers working at the subject restaurant lack tenure and experience.

Involving and Training Restaurant Employees

Restaurant employers must establish and provide continual and ongoing training for employees, supervisors, and managers from their first day of employment until their last.

This applies to all workers at all levels to ensure that everyone is aware of potential hazards and dangerous conditions relating to slip and falls, and how they can control and/or avoid them by using safe work procedures, floor cleaning, floor maintenance systems and procedures, and ongoing floor safety awareness.

No safety and health program will work without this commitment and involvement from management. The success of any safety management system pertaining to slip and fall and floor safety depends on careful planning and consistent execution by management and staff.

This means that restaurant owners, operators, and managers must take the time to analyze what needs to be accomplished to maintain a safe and healthy workplace environment. This includes the flooring surfaces and other tools of the trade to be used to maintain the safety of the flooring surfaces used by everyone working on the premises in various capacities, and frequenting the premises and thereby using the floors.

An action plan should be developed to attain safety goals and should involve employees as much as possible from the beginning.

Restaurant Management Has a Duty to Provide a Safe Environment

The restaurant industry's standard of care and duty is to create and maintain an environment that is safe for employees, customers, vendors, and others. Restaurant owners, managers, employers, and employees owe a duty to provide a safe environment to all who enter the restaurant.

With the Occupational Safety and Health Act (OSH Act) of 1970, Congress created the Occupational Safety and Health Administration (OSHA) to assure safe and healthful working conditions for working men and women by setting and enforcing standards and by providing training, outreach, education, and assistance.

Due to the previously mentioned common area/shared space inherent to the dining room areas/front of the house (FOH) of restaurants and most specifically the flooring surfaces used by all, these standards, training, outreach, and assistance ensure a safe and healthful environment that reasonably and customarily extends to everyone who enters and uses the premises and these common areas where the flooring surfaces are shared. The kitchen floor maintenance and care are also critically important to the front of the house floor conditions as the employees will be tracking contaminates from the kitchen out into the dining area.

Common Sense Plays a Critical Role in Risk Reduction and Safety in Restaurants

Common sense is one of the most important tools in recognizing and identifying hazards during any hazard analysis process, reducing risk, and creating and maintaining a safe, healthy, and secure flooring surface and walking and traversing environment.

I know lawyers hate the use of the term "common sense", but OSHA makes many references to common sense within its code. So, who am I to disagree with them?

Here are some examples: OSHA defines a worksite analysis as, "*A step-by-step common sense look at the workplace to find existing or potential hazards ….*"

OSHA also references common sense frequently throughout its documents, interpretations, explanations, codes, and guidelines. They even go so far as describing their standards as "common sense standards," their regulations as "common sense regulations," their

100 EXCUSES FOR ANYTHING

approach for implementation of the OSH Act as a "common sense approach;" and compliance with their standards and recommendations as "common-sense practices." They say, "*There's no excuse for an employer time and time again failing to supply such vital, common sense – and legally required – safeguards.*"

Restaurant Management Must Understand the Different Kinds of Recognized Hazards in the Restaurant Industry

OSHA defines the ways that a hazard qualifies as a recognized hazard. These include four forms of recognition:

Employer/Management Recognition - When there is actual employer or management knowledge or recognition of a hazardous condition. Evidence of this may be provided by written or oral statements made by the employer, other management or supervisors, and/or other employees and witnesses either before, during or after the incident. Obviously much of this information can be discovered and gleaned during deposition or trial testimony under oath when everyone feels more obligated and responsible to tell the truth, the whole truth, and nothing but the truth so please help them God.

Industry Recognition - When the employer's industry – in this case the restaurant, bar, food, and beverage industry – is aware of the existence of such a hazard and the specific kind of hazard either is, or reasonably should be, common knowledge to those working in or managing workers in the industry. For example, I can tell you with absolute certainty that the industry is very much aware of grease build-up both long and short term in restaurants, bars, and other food and beverage industry establishments and we have several tools of the trade designed specifically for dealing with grease build up and removing grease build up specific to our industry.

It is widely known that things as basic as slip and falls are leading causes of injury throughout the restaurant industry and, therefore there are several restaurant industry recognized hazards that everyone working in the industry does recognize or at least, everyone should reasonably recognize.

This is also true regarding the presence of offal – which is protein-based grease – on the floors of the restaurant.

Common Sense Recognition - When a hazard is so obvious and foreseeable that any reasonable person would have, or should have, recognized it, or any reasonable person with even the most basic amount, type, and kind of industry experience and training as either an employee or a management person should have recognized it.

Site Specific Recognized Hazard - This type of hazard is created when there is an existing activity, behavior, or condition that has the potential to cause injury or harm that is specific to a restaurant establishment (or group of restaurants, or type, kind, or style of menu), such as a unique environmental condition, building design, problematic traffic pattern, flooring issue, or other slip and fall hazard.

Restaurant Removed, Limited, Mitigated, Eliminated, Controlled, or Warned Of

A risk assessment is the initial step of a systematic method to control potential risks.

First, by identifying potential hazards in the restaurant (i.e., existing activities, behaviors, systems, processes, and/ or conditions that could cause potential harm or injury to persons). Then, analyzing or evaluating the risk(s) associated with each hazard (taking into consideration the potential for and the severity of harm or injury). Finally, deciding on what measures, if any, should be implemented to remove, limit, mitigate, eliminate, control, or warn of the hazard(s) to avoid injury or harm from occurring in the first place.

In much simpler terms, employers must take every reasonable and customary action to remove any potential danger for bodily harm or injury in their restaurant. Risk assessment is a tool for using experience, knowledge, skills, education, training, and just plain common sense to determine – if possible – what hazards exist in a restaurant. It provides a basis for considering alternative methods, actions, behaviors, systems, etc., to mitigate, eliminate, and/or control the risks involved.

The restaurant industry itself has many highly publicized and well-known dangers. Restaurant industry participants are required to take it upon themselves to constantly be on the lookout for hazards and dangerous conditions that may impact their customers, employees, vendors, and others. Doing anything to the contrary would be ill-advised, would not be prudent, would be out of compliance with OSHA, and would not meet the industry standard of reasonable and customary care. No risk is less important or less frequent than those associated with greasy flooring surfaces and the presence of protein-based grease, cooking oils, and offal.

LEAVING SPILLS UNGUARDED IS DANGEROUS

Is There...

Someone Standng by to Keep People Away?

A Sign Out to Drive Awareness?

Dry Grease on the Floor That Could Get Wet & Slick?

Don't Leave Spills on the Floor!

It's an Even Bigger Mess in Court...

Important to Remember: Limit, Mitigate, Eliminate, Control, Warn, and Address

Although cleaning the floors may seem like a simple task, there is a specific process that employees and managers need to keep in mind to properly clean and maintain it.

As I mentioned earlier, it's important that management remembers to:

- Select floor cleaning and maintenance products with proven slip resistance characteristics that are compatible with the flooring surfaces in a facility. Of note to me: The National Floor Safety Institute states that 10 out of the 18 products that they tested that were approved for tile floor cleaning actually made the tile floors more slippery after they were cleaned using the product.

- Provide proper signage and equipment to be used as a warning system during floor maintenance and quick reference for cleanup operations, such as safety cones, wet-floor signs, safety data sheets (SDS) and specifications regarding the slip-resistance level of products, safety posters, etc. Of note to me: OSHA's poster informing employees of their rights and responsibilities must be posted in a prominent location at all times to be in compliance and to meet industry standard.

- Implement carpet runners and mats that adhere to

OSHA and ADA (Americans with Disabilities Act) guidelines.

- Consider foreseeable conditions, such as the weather (rain, mud, dirt, sand, snow, etc.); provide employee access to slip resistant footwear and make it a requirement.
- Provide for regular site safety and health inspections.

There are also certain factors to remember considering a cleaning product:

- Detergents or surfactants: increase penetration of water-soluble soils and contaminants.
- Emulsifiers, soaps and degreasers: help to dissolve and suspend fat-soluble soils. Using too little will be insufficient for removing grease; using too much may dissolve the grease but leave a slippery residue behind.
- Biological agents: blend naturally occurring bacteria with powerful enzymes for efficient, effective, safe cleaning and removal of excessive grease.
- Caustics and acids (harsh or corrosive agents): chemically break down and strip contaminants.
- Other additives and agents for slip-resistance, shining, sealing, fragrance, drying, and disinfectants can help to minimize the chances of slip and falls.

Clean mops are most effective. Mops can become contaminated quickly and spread grease and soil instead of removing it. It is restaurant industry standard to:

- Use clean mops; replace, remove or thoroughly clean dirty mops. Refer to the manufacturer for best cleaning instructions.

- Utilize dirt screens or water contaminate-separating agents for cleaner water in the mop bucket(s).

- Utilize several mop buckets to have separate compartments for dirty mop wringing, dirty mop rinsing, and cleaning solution dipping. Floor squeegees may be used to spread cleaning solution to help minimize cross-contamination.

The Restaurant Industry Standard Process for Cleaning the Floors Must Be Followed

Management and employees must understand the industry standards for keeping floors hazard-free for the safety of guests and employees that are simple, manageable, and critical to the well-being of everybody involved.

These standards used to be – and still are required to be – the norm, rather than the exception, and well understood by both employer and employee. These basic restaurant industry standards, policies, procedures, and protocols for cleaning floors that restaurants should do every day include:

- Sweep the floor well with a dry broom to remove debris and then rinse the floor with hot water.

- Mop the floor with an enzymatic degreaser. There is a specific type of bacteria in the cleaner and the degreaser produces enzymes that break up the grease. Then, the specific type of bacteria in the cleaner consumes what the enzymes were designed to break down. It is critical that this is done correctly, and that the proper product is selected.

- Rinse the floor again with hot water.
- Add the floor cleaner and mop the floor with a clean mop. It is critical that this is done correctly, and the proper products have been selected.
- Rinse the floor again with hot water.
- Use a deck brush to thoroughly clean the floor surface before a final rinse and at every previous stage where a mop was used. It is also critical that these are used every time to avoid a buildup of the protein-based offal-grease, and the brushing is done thoroughly. Think of the process of how a man using hair gels or cremes must scrub his own hair vigorously when attempting to get men's haircare product out of his hair.
- Give the floor a final rinse with hot water.
- Dry the floor with a dry mop or a blower.

And while cleaning, restaurants should remember to:

- Always choose the best time to clean (when other employees, customers, etc. are not around — unless, of course, they are cleaning up a spill) to allow for longer periods of drying time and the least chance that someone might slip or fall on the wet, freshly washed flooring surface.

- Set up appropriate warning/caution signage to keep others away while cleaning or washing floors or getting up spills or wet spots.

- Provide safe access around the work area when others are present.

- Prior to cleaning or washing the floor, remove excess dirt or grease by wiping, scraping, and/or sweeping. This makes cleaning easier and helps reduce the likelihood of contaminants from spreading.

- Avoid contacting surrounding restaurant equipment and machinery with water, cleaning agents, cleaning tools, and equipment.

- Use only the designated tools and cleaning materials for the particular area/zone of the restaurant that a person is currently cleaning (check for labels and color codes).

- Rinse floors after scrubbing.

- Use a wet vacuum, floor machine or squeegee to force excess liquids into floor drains and speed up the drying process.

- Clean smaller areas/sections of the floor at a time for easier, more manageable clean up and to prevent cross-contamination.

- Start by cleaning the less soiled/contaminated areas; finish that area first, then proceed to the next dirtiest until complete (be sure to keep drainage in mind).

Most of the time when I am inspecting a restaurant that has failed to clean protein-based offal-grease off the floor, I discover that something (often many things) in this process were not followed correctly or consistently.

Like I mentioned earlier, improper or partial cleaning of the floors actually makes the buildup and effect of offal worse rather than better. These cleaning procedures are simple steps, but critical for keeping a restaurant safe for everyone.

Restaurants Should Color Code the Cleaning Materials

No, not all mops should be used for the same purpose or in the same area. Cleaning the front of house is very different than cleaning the back of house, and the tools that are used to clean each surface need to be kept separate.

When it comes to grease buildup, the floors are going to have a worse buildup of offal in the kitchen than they will in the front of house. If employees use the same mop for both surfaces, they're bound to accidentally or apathetically spread the kitchen grease onto the floor of the dining room.

That means managers need to ensure that there are separate mops, mop buckets, deck brushes, squeegees, dry mops, and other cleaning materials for each area and train the employees to use them separately.

The cleaning tools used for each area need to be color coded, each clearly marking whether a tool is used for the front of house or back of house. Most commonly, one set is labeled with red tape or tags and the other with blue. It is important that employees do not mix the designated flooring surfaces that each mop or deck brush cleans, otherwise the buildup of grease can just move places instead of being removed.

Figure Eights Are Essential to Mopping Restaurant Floors

The art of doing a figure eight doesn't just belong on an ice rink. And if a restaurant employee doesn't do his/her figure eights while mopping, the floor just might turn into an ice rink.

It is not enough for managers or employees to simply run a mop over the flooring surface in order to clean the floor properly and it is not enough to simply move it back and forth in rows. Mopping motions are not like mowing the front lawn. That mop is designed to clean up dirt and it's going to need some elbow grease to do it.

And if an employee is only moving the mop back and forth – towards and away from him/her – then there will not to be enough pressure on the mop for it to fully clean the floors. In fact, it might make them worse.

That's why those who clean the floor need to move the mop in a figure eight right in front of them. By doing so, they can keep a constant pressure on the handle that actually lifts and removes dirt and thoroughly cleans the floor. It's not just enough to go through the motions and steps necessary to clean the floor, they need to be done *right.*

The Stranger Danger of the Restaurant Spill Creep

No, the spill creep isn't a 1970s serial killer or a 1980s horror movie character, it's just another hazard that can turn someone's lunchbreak into a horror movie.

The spill creep is simply what it sounds like…a spill that creeps.

That sneaky little spill of little Suzie's sweet tea may have been small when it poured off the table, but it can quickly and carelessly be spread out and mopped across the floor by an ignorant, apathetic, lazy, or lackadaisical employee who thinks that spreading the spill out will make it less hazardous. It won't.

Instead, the wet area that now re-hydrates the offal on the floor gets spread to a much bigger area like twelve feet instead of the twelve inches it was originally covering and creeps across the floor to make the rest of it much more slippery.

The puddle may be gone, but the hazard has gotten worse.

And if you notice, spreading out the spill to let it creep across the floor is not part of the industry standard for keeping floors safe, but too many employees assume it is when they should be taught the proper and thorough ways to clean and guard a spill.

The concept of the spill creep should be no stranger to restaurant management, and if it is, they will be no stranger to it when they get served a lawsuit over a slip and fall.

The Grotesque and Gory Spill Splatter on Restaurant Floors

The spill splatter, much like the spill creep, is another sinister – but simple – issue that causes slips and falls to occur. Restaurants must be aware of them to keep the floors safe.

The spill splatter happens…when spills splatter. Complicated definition, I know. But all too often employees are not thinking about where the liquid is going when Uncle Bill spills his Diet Coke in one spot, but when the liquid hits the floor it still splatters to many more spots, and many times several feet away from the original spill location.

Think about the last violent movie you saw where someone's

head got blown off and the brains and blood went everywhere. Yes, that's graphic, but that image is pretty much how any spill splatter works. And just like the fake blood the studio used to splatter on the wall and make the whole movie theater cringe, that Diet Coke does the same splattering on the floor.

The hazard, then, is still there after the ignorant, apathetic, lazy, or lackadaisical employee comes to clean the one spot where the Diet Coke spilled and leaves the other smaller droplets, and miniature puddles, splattered where they lie.

That's like cleaning up the brains off the wall but leaving the rest of the blood splatters on the edges. When employees just clean one spot, that splatter goes unnoticed by them and unnoticed by the unsuspecting customer who ends up slipping on that splatter an hour later.

That means that in a true culture of safety, those who clean the floors aren't just worried about the one spot where they saw the spill, they're worried about the safety of the whole floor, which includes the spill splatter.

The Terrible Idea of Hand Towels in Restaurant Bathrooms

Splatter can come from more than spills too. All too often it comes simply from people drying their hands in the bathroom. You may think that using fewer paper towels makes the planet safer – and maybe it does – but running out of them makes the floor a lot more dangerous. Whether in the bathroom or in the kitchen, when the paper towels run out and nobody replaces them, employees or customers find their own way to dry their hands that puts the water right on the floor.

Think about it, what do you do when your freshly washed hands are dripping-wet and you walk up to the dispenser to find the bathroom out of paper towels? If you're like the rest of us (and you probably are) then you shake off your hands and wipe what's left on your pants and walk out. So does everyone else and employees do the same thing when the kitchen runs out of paper towels. And all that water shaken off of their hands winds up on the floor ready to re-hydrate the offal.

And to make things worse, that spot where people dry their hands is usually right in the pathway of the door, so now the droplets are right in the walkway for people to slip on when they were just trying to go pee. Or, if they don't slip, the water is there for them to track it out into the rest of the restaurant and wet the grease on the floor elsewhere. It's a simple problem, but it's a major factor behind far too many catastrophic injuries. To keep the premises safe, restaurants need to remember to both clean the bathroom areas and check them often.

They Took Hand Towels Out of Restaurants and Made the Idea Worse

Some restaurants have recognized the problem of hand towels and people shaking their hands off onto the floor and decided to come up with a solution: to install hand dryers that just blow all the water off of their hands and onto the floor for them. That way, they don't have to worry about supplying paper towels and the mess on the floor gets even worse!

But seriously, I want to have a talk with whoever thought that hand dryers were the proper solution to shaken water droplets creating hazards on the floor. It may feel like all those hand dryers do is warm and evaporate the water off of your hands into thin air like magic, but in reality, most of it is getting blown directly onto the floor and creating the same hazard right in the walkway of the bathroom, bound to injure someone walking by or get tracked through the restaurant to injure someone elsewhere.

The best solution then, whether trying to make a restaurant safer from empty paper towel bins or from hand dryers, is to get the hand dryers that require a person's hands to be inserted into a confined space and blown on from both sides. Often referred to as "hands down" or "vertical" hand dryers, these have a design that catches the water that comes off a person's hands and ensures far less of a mess on the floor. Restaurant owners may think that those are too fancy for them to be worth it, but they won't after someone's Grandpa slips on his way out of their bathroom because the hand dryers made a mess.

It's a good thing that our culture expects people to wash their hands, but in a culture of safety it should be expected that restaurants keep the bathrooms safe from the aftermath.

The Problem of Pee (Urine) Splatter

It's not just the clean water from people's hands that makes the bathroom floors dangerous, it's the human wastewater being urinated out…and splattered on the floor by the customers. Especially if the floors are greasy, pee splatter by urinals and toilets can make the floor not only gross, but dangerously slippery. So much so that customers are at risk of slipping and catastrophically injuring themselves in the middle of relieving themselves.

And it's a bigger problem than the fact that so many men don't aim well when they pee (yes, that's part of it, but no one that I'm aware of is fixing that problem any time soon). All too often the bathrooms are not designed to contain the splatter of urine, even if the aim is good. Urinals that go all the way to the floor do virtually nothing to keep that splatter contained, urinals that are raised up the wall and have rounded edges help contain it some, and when a urinal includes a urinal mat it helps contain the pee even better. Restaurants need to take into account how to get the best urinal for maximum pee containment.

When men pee in toilets, on the other hand, the bowl is not designed in the kind of shape that can catch the urine splatter from such a high distance and the splatter still gets on the floor. So yes, if you were wondering, pee splatter is a predominately male problem. But it does occur in women's bathrooms as well.

For restaurant management, that means cleaning the bathrooms regularly is critical to the safety of the floors. Especially if offal has gotten in the bathroom from the air vents or foot traffic, it doesn't take much urine or water to make the whole floor extremely dangerous.

Transition Mats and Restaurant Floors

Transition mats are also critical to keep from tracking grease or water from the kitchen to the dining room. Their purpose is to catch the material on the bottom of employees' shoes and hold it until cleaned. It's a simple job, but it takes more than just throwing one down to get it to function well and ensure the floor's safety.

In order to place transition mats properly, there needs to be two placed next to each other, one inside the kitchen door and the other outside coming into the dining room. That way, there's a double catch of grease and a restaurant doesn't wind up with one side of the doorway still becoming extremely slippery. Employees need to be trained not to roll carts over the mats because the weight can catch the grease that's down in the mat and roll the grease from the wheels all over it, turning both the cart's pathway and the mats into hazards.

Most importantly, transition mats are only useful if they are regularly kept clean. Otherwise, they become just a holding area for employees to pick up more offal on their way to and from the kitchen. Like any other tool, transition mats need to be used right, and just because a restaurant has one or two doesn't mean it is using and maintaining them properly.

Transition mats are important safety tools for the front and back ingress and egress doors as well, but one must be clear on exactly how to secure them, clean and maintain them, place them, and manage them for it to be an improved safety environment because of them.

How to Look for Offal When Inspecting a Restaurant

When conducting the "managers walk" – or when anyone is inspecting a restaurant – looking for signs of offal buildup needs to be a priority in determining the safety of the restaurant. I have personally conducted far too many site inspections where the signs of the four biggest hazards were everywhere in the form of offal buildup, which told me everything I needed to know about the culture of safety set by the leadership there.

The obvious sign of offal buildup is when you first walk into a restaurant and the floor immediately feels either slippery or sticky, depending on the moisture in the room and the length of time the offal was present and allowed to mature and age. But there are other, more subtle signs that point to the danger of offal becoming an unexpected hazard in a single moment.

Some of these signs include:

- A buildup of grease in the grout lines of a tile floor, both in the kitchen and the dining room.
- Dark marks on the baseboards where a greasy mop has run up against the wall.
- A higher buildup of offal under surfaces that are not cleaned as regularly or thoroughly such as kitchen equipment, tables and chairs, or points of sale.
- A buildup in or on the air vents where offal has gotten into the ventilation system.
- A grease buildup or discoloration on the cleaning equipment itself such as a yellow mop bucket, the wheels of the mop bucket, the squeegees, or other tools that have retained grease.
- A greasy feeling on the tabletops, menus, or other dining room objects.
- Transition mats, especially if they have not been cleaned, can be found to have a buildup of grease or even pools of it within the mats.
- The backdoor, where employees normally roll grease

out to dispose of it, can show signs of tracking it from their feet or from a cart.

- The concrete outside the main entry can often be discolored from where customers have tracked grease from inside the building or even outside the building. Especially if there is a discolored line where you can directly trace the pathway customers took when they came in or left, it becomes obvious that they were tracking from an offal buildup inside or grease and grime of a different type from the outside.

Those are still not all of the signs, but you get the idea. Restaurants should understand that the same things I would look for in a site inspection ought to be the same things they look for all the time to ensure that their customers and employees are as safe as possible.

Restaurant Employers Must Use 'What-If' Hazard Analysis

Restaurant industry employers are best advised to use the 'what-if' method of training in order to attempt to reduce risk, prevent incidents before they happen, and create and maintain a safe place for customers and employees.

This 'what-if' methodology is used to analyze the overall restaurant premises and operating processes and specifically the floor safety, cleaning, maintenance, and establishment upkeep in an effort to identify existing or potential hazards, problems, dangerous conditions, and possible accident scenarios.

This method usually requires a brainstorming approach by a review group (many times consisting of restaurant employees, safety committee members, supervisory personnel, owners, multi-unit managers, general operations managers, risk managers etc.) that are familiar with the restaurant operating processes (systems, equipment, tasks, tools, procedures, etc.) used in the workplace that are to be analyzed.

The committee or group is tasked with raising questions or concerns about what could happen if deviations in the operating processes develop, or failures occur that lead to flooring surfaces becoming slippery, or more dangerous. These questions are presented as 'what-if' scenarios, as in, "what if we notice an oily film build-up on the floors?" or "what if an employee or customer can't see that step down?" These 'what-if' scenarios should lead to problem-solving hazards to prevent danger such as, "what tools do we need to keep the floors walkable and safe?"

These issues may also be presented as an expression of concern such as, "I worry about what will happen if we run out of floor degreaser over the weekend," or "I'm afraid of a scenario where a child might run across this floor when they are running to the bathroom." This methodology is based on the premise that a hazard, dangerous condition, or accident should not occur if there are no deviations (alterations/

changes) from the process as it is intended to function or operate on a regular basis.

This form of analysis usually begins with a visual inspection. At each step of the operating process or premises being analyzed, the team identifies possible accident scenarios, various consequences or outcomes, and the existing safeguards that the restaurant currently has in place. The next step is to write down the 'what-if' questions or concerns that arise regarding safety, health, and security. Then, divide the 'what-ifs' into specific categories or areas of the restaurant to be addressed by the hazard analysis team. In most cases, this analysis can be conducted with as little as one or two people, unless a complex process is being examined which may require more.

Next, the team members suggest possible risk reductions, recommendations, and corrective actions that may be taken to help prevent these accidental 'what-if' scenarios from becoming a reality or, at the very least, reducing the severity of the outcome if the hazard itself cannot be eliminated completely. Finally, the team must deliberate and arrive at a consensus for the best action to be taken and see to it that the chosen action is implemented.

The 'what-if' questions and their answers are key elements to creating a hazard assessment analysis and report, which can be an extremely useful tool in training restaurant employees and operating personnel on the possible hazards of the particular operation and the safety of the floors in every part of the restaurant. 'What-ifs' are also a great training tool for lower level, less experienced management personnel such as team leaders, shift managers, and assistant managers to help them learn what to do during certain incidents and events that require quick reaction, or when they are unable to get in touch with a supervisor to provide insight or direction after someone has slipped in the bathroom and someone needs to call the ambulance.

'What-ifs' are also used for training employees for all kinds of different risk scenarios that could occur in a restaurant where someone could get injured, harmed, sickened, maimed, or killed.

This training should also include providing employees with contact information and who to call in the event of an incident.

Restaurants Must Provide Competent Person Oversight

The term "competent person" is referenced many times throughout OSHA standards and documents and used regularly across the restaurant industry. OSHA and the industry participants generally define the term as someone who is capable of identifying existing and predictable hazards in the surroundings or working conditions which are unsanitary, hazardous, or dangerous to employees and

customers, and who has the authorization to take prompt corrective measures to eliminate them.

I think we can all agree that floor safety is a very basic responsibility for all employees and that things like sweeping and mopping floors and looking for floor-related slip risks and fall risks should be a key component that fits into everyone's wheelhouse. Employees should be trained from the start of their first day about the importance of keeping floors clean and dry and removing any and all drips, leaks, spills, and slippery spots quickly and immediately upon noticing them.

In practical applications, a competent person may also be required to have other skillsets such as the ability to manage and train other employees – that seems so basic you wouldn't think that I would have to say it, but trust me, from experience, I can tell you that I do.

OSHA, of course, allows room for restaurant industry employers, the industry itself, and the experts conducting business across the industry the use of common sense to define more precisely what a competent person represents in their specific industry. Criteria for determining such are typically based on how a restaurant employee performs and the level of experience, training, knowledge, and skills of the employee as perceived by the restaurant employer or supervisor.

Regardless of how it is determined, designating an individual as a competent person, and putting him or her in charge in any situation, must help protect the workers and must not endanger their safety, health, and security or the safety, health, and security of others. It is important to note that when an employer (owner, manager, operator, etc.) designates an individual as a competent person, it does not mean that the words "competent person" become his/her job title or a part of his/her job title. For instance, he/she may carry the job title of Assistant Manager or Shift Manager and the words "competent person" will most likely never be included in his/her job title. Being competent should just be a part of the job.

It is reasonable and customary throughout the restaurant industry for those chosen by their employer to be responsible for management and training and/or oversight of employees, people, and/or the premises to be competent as it pertains to safety, health, and security—regardless of their title, time on the job, or level of compensation. Therefore, they must be capable of identifying the existing and potential safety, health, and security hazards on the restaurant premises.

In addition, they must be given the authority to take whatever corrective action or actions may be necessary to create a safe, healthy, and secure workplace and premises for both employees and customers. Such authority includes minimizing a hazard, removing a hazard, or, if necessary, not allowing certain work activities or customer activities to happen at all if that is the best option to remove employees, customers, and others from the perceived or imminent danger. These requirements are highly important to note due to the many different levels of management necessary to cover all the hours of operation and the various functions and areas of a restaurant.

If there is a restaurant employer, owner, manager, etc., who has given someone the title of manager, trainer, team leader, or a title of any kind granting him or her the authority to manage, lead, or oversee other employees or the restaurant premises – or even if they have not actually given him or her the official title, but have given him or her the authority of manager, trainer, etc. (either temporarily, such as acting closing manager for a night or two, or permanently) – then whether they know it or not, they have automatically designated him/her to be a competent person. That said, it must be made certain that he/she meets the OSHA standard and the restaurant industry standard of competent as it pertains to management oversight and safety, health, and security.

Of particular note: each year the absence of competent persons is among the most frequently cited violations by OSHA. This oversight results in a significant number of accidents and fatalities across the restaurant and bar industry. Lack of competent management oversight tends to result in a significant number of incidents where employees, customers, vendors, or others end up being injured, harmed, sickened, maimed, or killed in restaurants every year.

Restaurant Management Are Expected to Create and Maintain a Culture of Safety

The reasonable and customary restaurant industry standard of care is for management to create and maintain a safety-first mentality among all of the employees.

This includes creating an environment of basic policies, procedures, operating systems, safety protocols, safety rules, training programs and protocols, and standards in written form which are also upheld and maintained in verbal communication, as well as executed on a day-to-day, regular basis. This is commonly referred to across the industry as a culture of safety.

To comply, the culture of safety must apply to the entire organization and all of the employees working within it to offer a reasonable and customary level of caution and to ensure that prudence, as it pertains to safety and health for all, is regularly and consistently exercised.

In the restaurant industry, to create and maintain a culture of safety, many individual things must happen. Those things include, but are not limited to:

- written policies and procedures.
- training in a language and style that each employee can individually understand.
- conducting continual and ongoing training for each employee during the entire length of their employment.

- conducting regularly scheduled safety meetings.
- providing every employee with safety meeting notes, communications, and bulletins.
- providing safety, health, and hazard communication to all employees in various forms.
- doing incident reports and incident investigations in a timely manner after an incident does occur wherein someone was injured, harmed, sickened, maimed or killed.
- providing staff the necessary tools of the trade to safely do their assigned jobs and tasks.
- conducting regular and periodic site safety audits and hazard assessments.
- having an open-door policy so that employees at every level can voice their concerns and point out what they see as hazards and dangerous conditions.
- having management and ownership talk about safety, health, and security regularly.
- creating an environment where all employees have a reasonable degree of caution and prudence as it pertains to safety, health, and security to recognize, eliminate, mitigate and/or warn of hazards and dangerous conditions that may exist anywhere on the restaurant premises and anywhere the restaurant's operations and/or business happens.

Once again, creating any environment or any culture to

the contrary of this long-standing, safety-first mentality is ill-advised and is neither prudent nor up to restaurant industry standard.

Written Policies and Procedures Are Required in Restaurants

The reasonable and customary restaurant industry standard is to provide every employee with written policies, procedures, and practices pertaining to safety, health, and security.

These written policies and procedures must be provided in a language and vocabulary that each employee can understand. They ensure consistency in the event of employee turnover, turnover of safety trainers or managers, and/or emergencies, and also ensure that specific information regarding safety, health, and day-to-day operations is made available to all employees.

Additionally, written programs can be offered as proof of the employer and employee commitment to each standard and operating system. "As the size of the worksite or the complexity of a hazardous operation increases ... the need for written guidance increases to ensure clear communication of policies and priorities as well as consistent and fair application of rules."

Management should "ensure that all employees, including themselves, have clearly written safety and health responsibilities included within their job description, with appropriate authority to carry out those responsibilities."

According to OSHA and restaurant industry guidelines, it is important for restaurant industry employers to have a written plan that details the workplace's general safety and health program, and it really should contain five basic program elements:

- Management Leadership and Employee Involvement
- Worksite Analysis
- Hazard Prevention and Control
- Training
- Hazard Communication Systems

The reasonable and customary restaurant industry standard is for employees to be provided the Hazard Communications via written fliers, bulletins, and documentation placed in the employee file after provided notification.

Hazard Communication is an OSHA training requirement required by law. The Hazard Communication standard improves the quality and consistency of hazard information in the workplace. This standard is one of the top ten most frequent OSHA citations for Eating and Drinking Establishments.

Written training and "documentation" can also supply an answer to one of the first questions an incident investigator will ask. "Did the employee receive adequate training to do the job?" This is also one of the first questions a restaurant owner or manager would and should reasonably and customarily ask when an incident occurs.

Safety Meetings Are Required in Restaurants

The reasonable and customary restaurant industry standard is for management to conduct regular safety meetings that include all employees.

The operating system traditionally implemented across the restaurant industry is that safety meetings occur on either a monthly or a quarterly basis and that all employees are present or, in cases where all employees cannot be present, those employees are disseminated information regarding the safety meeting via notes, fliers, and direct communication. Files are traditionally kept of safety meeting agendas and those in attendance.

Safety Tools and Tools of the Trade Must be Maintained

The reasonable and customary restaurant industry standard is for employees to be provided safety, health, and operational tools necessary for them to do the assigned jobs.

OSHA requires, as part of employer responsibilities, to, "Make sure employees have and use safe tools and equipment and properly maintain this equipment." As it pertains to floor safety, floor cleanliness, floor maintenance, and floor care in a restaurant there are certain tools that are critically important in order to reasonably meet the standard to do the job.

They include but are not limited to the following: floor cleaner (various approved kinds, types, and brands), floor degreaser (various approved kinds, types, and brands), mops, mop buckets, squeegees, deck brushes, hot water, cold water, slippery when wet floor caution signs, mop sink, mop and broom storage rack or unit, and floor mats (various approved kinds, types, and brands).

Employers and Employees Must Use Tools for Their Intended Purpose

The reasonable and customary restaurant industry standard is for employees at every level to use equipment, furniture, fixtures, facility, and tools for their reasonably identified, acceptable, and intended purpose.

They should not use the tools of the trade for purposes other than what the manufacturer intended them to be used for, or in a manner that would be reasonably and prudently deemed to be an unintended purpose which may create a hazard, a dangerous condition, or a higher than customary level of risk of someone being injured, harmed, sickened, maimed, and/ or killed.

OSHA provides the following definition for "identified" (as

applied to equipment): "*Approved as suitable for the specific purpose, function, use, environment, or application, where described in a particular requirement.*"

Restaurant Managers Must Conduct Safety Inspections and Know the Recognized Hazards

The reasonable and customary restaurant industry standard is to conduct regular and ongoing worksite and job hazard analysis – commonly referred to as safety audits or safety inspections across the restaurant industry.

Safety inspections are traditionally conducted by several different levels of management and/or competent persons at regular time and calendar intervals consisting of differing levels of detail and documentation on a continual, hourly, pre-daypart, daily, weekly, monthly, quarterly, and annual basis. These safety inspections consist of walking the entire property inside and out, while reviewing all aspects of the physical facility including furniture, fixtures, and equipment, and the complete analysis of each restaurant position's job duties and responsibilities.

This series of safety inspections is conducted in order to make a reasonable, customary, and prudent attempt to recognize potential hazards and dangerous conditions, and then take the reasonable, customary, prudent, and necessary actions to resolve potential hazards and dangerous conditions before an incident occurs and someone becomes injured, harmed, sickened, maimed or killed.

Potential hazards and dangerous conditions cannot be consistently identified and resolved, and injuries cannot be consistently prevented without first identifying and recognizing them. This process is also commonly referred to as site and job hazard analysis.

Restaurant managers and other competent persons acting on behalf of the restaurant owner must be trained to be able to consider and identify reasonably foreseeable conditions and conduct regular site safety and health inspections with a prudent and professional level of caution as a part of their professional responsibilities. During these inspections, any recognized potential hazard and/or dangerous condition must be removed, mitigated, or at the very least, proper warnings, cautions, and safety measures must be put in place for the safety and health of employees, customers, vendors, and all who enter the premises.

Restaurant Managers Must Incorporate Hazard Control Measures When Necessary

Information obtained from a job hazard analysis is useless unless hazard control measures recommended in the analysis are incorporated into the tasks.

Managers should recognize that not all hazard controls are equal, as some are more effective than others at reducing risk. The order of precedence and effectiveness of hazard control is the following:

1. Engineering Controls:

- Elimination/minimization of the hazard – designing the facility, equipment, or process to remove the hazard, or substituting processes, equipment, materials, or other factors to lessen the hazard:

- Enclosure of the hazard – this should be the first step when seeing a floor hazard. Go stand by it and block it off until a team member can come help and resolve the issue at hand.

- Isolation of the hazard

- Removal or redirection of the hazard

2. Administrative Controls:

- Written operating procedures, work permits, and safe work practices

- Exposure time limitations

- Monitoring the use of highly hazardous materials

- Alarms, signs, and warnings
- Buddy system
- Training

3. Personal Protective Equipment...is acceptable as a control method in the following circumstances:

- When engineering controls are not feasible or do not totally eliminate the hazard.
- While engineering controls are being developed.
- When safe work practices do not provide sufficient additional protection.
- During emergencies when engineering controls may not be feasible.

Restaurant Managers Must Do Routine Inspections

Routine safety, health, and security walkthrough inspections should be conducted by top management, safety and health staff, members of safety committees, etc.

These inspections are a good way to audit the program and can help a person identify areas that need to be addressed. They also keep safety, health, and security efforts visible and top-of-mind. It is the restaurant industry standard for management and employees to be

responsible for conducting scheduled inspections (per shift, daily, weekly, monthly, etc.) in specific areas of the restaurant.

Things to look for during inspections differ depending on the type or kind of incident that we may be referring to but for this category it looks like the following:

- Toilets: should flush properly and completely; all parts should be attached and accounted for; look for cracks; toilet should be stable (firmly attached to the floor).
- Tiles: loose or cracked tiles, grout, and caulking may indicate a water leak issue within the walls.
- Mold and Mildew: indicate standing moisture problems.
- Faucets, Fixtures, and Valves: check for leaks and proper turn on/off.

And so much more.

Restaurant Managers Must Do Worksite Analysis and Routine Building Inspections

Routine building and facility inspections combined with preventative maintenance can become a much simpler process when conducted in a systematic manner.

Facility inspections must be performed on a regular and timely basis. As it is for many other routine tasks in the restaurant industry, so it is for facility inspections in that it is customary to develop an inspection checklist to help the restaurant owners/managers in identifying and keeping accurate records of any recognized problems to facilitate prompt repair and maintenance.

In addition, it is highly recommended that a manager begins by hiring a professional commercial building inspector and/ or risk manager that focuses on operations, systems, risk management, and training that will perform his/her inspection(s) in accordance with local, state, and county building codes and /or industry standards (to create a baseline from which to form a checklist).

This should provide a restaurant with a comprehensive assessment of the current condition of the restaurant facility from a visual perspective pertaining to all the reasonably accessible structural elements and from a safety, health, and security perspective. The checklist should include all areas of the exterior and interior of the facility.

Restaurant owners and operators have a duty and responsibility to ensure that their facility is safe for human occupation and conducting routine inspections helps immensely with this duty and responsibility. Performing this kind of preventative risk management and maintenance is reasonable and customary throughout the restaurant industry.

Restaurant Managers Must Complete Incident Reports and Conduct Incident Investigation

Being vigilant about the incidents that occur and what caused them is an integral part of preventing them from happening again to either another guest or another employee.

The reasonable and customary restaurant industry standard when an incident does occur is for:

- onsite management at the time of the incident to fill out a thorough and complete incident report that includes photographs, witness statements (including customers and employees), information about the injured party, a statement from the injured party, and any other reasonably pertinent information and evidence that can be collected; and,

- for general management, senior-level management, and/or owner to conduct a thorough and complete incident investigation of the subject location at the incident site each, and every time an incident involving an employee, a customer, a vendor, or other person occurs.

These two long-standing, industry standard operating systems and safety-related protocols are conducted by site management immediately after the incident in a reasonable, customary, and prudent attempt to determine what caused the incident to occur; for the general management, senior-level management, and/or owners to determine what, if any, hazards or dangerous conditions existed or led to the incident and to determine what, if anything, needs to be done to resolve any potential hazard or dangerous condition to ensure someone else does not become injured, harmed, sickened, maimed, or killed.

An industry professional (restaurant management and/or owner) should most certainly understand that the products (foods and beverages) that are bought, sold, and served in restaurants go directly inside of the bodies of those customers that are served – the work product by those in the restaurant industry is a consumable, and nearly every man, woman, and child in the United States consumes it at one time or another.

Because of this – and the hospitality and service functions associated with the restaurant industry – the restaurant industry is a highly personal relationship between restaurant employee and restaurant customer and is like few other industries in existence. This unique relationship leads to the reasonable expectation by restaurant customers and patrons to believe that restaurant managers, owners, and employees take the reasonably prudent and necessary steps to protect them (the customers) from being injured, harmed, sickened, maimed, and/or killed. And it especially should lead to restaurant managers and owners to exercise caution, prudence, and concern at every possible turn – which is reasonable and reasonably expected – and the trust that they have been given.

Taking the reasonable and customary actions to recognize, eliminate, mitigate, and/or warn of hazards and dangerous conditions that may exist anywhere on the premises is an integral part of accomplishing OSHA standards, HACCP standards, and industry safety, health and security standards nationwide.

As previously stated, some of the components to HACCP pertaining to incidents and recognizing and eliminating hazards (to comply with the restaurant industry standard of care) are to establish corrective actions and establish recordkeeping procedures. This cannot be done without thoroughly understanding the situation.

I do not believe that restaurants, restaurant managers, and restaurant owners can accomplish this level of duty, due diligence, caution, prudence, and standard of care without conducting thorough and complete incident reports and incident investigations after anyone has been injured, harmed, sickened, maimed, and/or killed on the premises to protect the next individual that could possibly be injured, harmed, sickened, maimed, and/or killed.

CHAPTER 5
If It Can Happen to Them, It Can Happen to You

M*AKE NO MISTAKE* about it, restaurants can be very dangerous places for those who are untrained or untrustworthy.

And they can be very dangerous places for those who enter establishments where the people in charge (the various levels of management and the owner) are not trained on basic industry standards, policies and procedures, operating systems, and safety and health guidelines – especially those pertaining to something as basic as floor safety, floor cleaning, floor maintenance and floor upkeep and, therefore, are not able to reasonably, customarily, and prudently recognize and resolve hazards and dangerous conditions.

I love the restaurant industry, and so does the majority of the US population, but together we must demand a higher level of performance as it pertains to safety, health, and security for us all, and I believe that starts with more basic day-to-day operational training and oversight with something as straight forward and simple as the flooring surfaces that we all walk on.

From hands-on experience, I can tell you that the number of incidents occurring each year in restaurants and bars across America is truly mind-boggling. And for those of us that deal with them, and the people that they directly and indirectly impact, it's heartbreaking. These slip and fall incidents, accidents, events, and occurrences happen to employees, vendors, independent contractors, and customers from nearly every walk of life.

And if it can happen to them, it can happen to you, your spouse, your child, your parent, or your loved one at any time. The unfortunate truth is that the vast majority of these incidents are preventable.

These incidents change the lives of nearly everyone involved, from the person or persons harmed (the victims), to the manager or owner responsible for the premises. In some instances, they are damaged physically, mentally, and emotionally for years to come, and in many cases, they are left scarred for the remainder of their lives. These incidents also impact the lives of those who are forced by pure happenstance to watch them take place: family members, other customers, employees, and witnesses.

Just imagine your own loved one walking back from the bathroom one second and suddenly in the next sprawled on the floor with a fractured skull. That memory doesn't go away for those who see it.

Restaurants, that are otherwise reasonably viable and substantially profitable businesses, are having to close their doors due to the overwhelmingly negative impact of these types of slip and fall incidents that occur on their premises.

Right now, at this very moment, many restaurateurs are dealing with serious court cases and overwhelming litigation matters, all the while watching their hopes and dreams of owning and operating a successful restaurant go up in smoke. Their dreams have devolved into a nightmare of litigation and financial loss; sadly, it is mostly due to their complete lack of awareness of hazardous and dangerous conditions and a lack of the necessary training required to reduce risks and prevent these types of slip and fall incidents from happening on their premises in the first place.

Once these cases have been adjudicated, and in many instances well prior to the final ruling, the dreams of many will instead turn into life altering nightmares of epic proportions, from the likes of which they may never fully recover.

Unfortunately, it seems, if anyone is in the restaurant industry long enough, one day he/she will most likely be "served". No, I'm not referring to lunch or dinner. I'm talking about the likelihood that the owner will be served a lawsuit or an insurance claim that could forever change the course of that business and the remainder of his/her life.

In the blink of an eye, when one least expects it, one single slip or fall incident, or a history of them, could result in the owner and the business being liable for claims, damages, and attorney's fees amounting to hundreds of thousands or even tens of millions of dollars.

All it takes is for one judge or jury to rule that someone was not operating the restaurant according to reasonable and customary industry standards, or in compliance with the law, or that they were somehow derelict in their duties, or negligent in their actions and the gig is up and the pockets will be emptied.

So, the real question to those in charge must be this: Why would any person responsible for a restaurant make it any easier for the lawyers to wring them dry by failing to take every necessary precaution ahead of time?

If they haven't already, owners, supervisors, and managers need to step up and start protecting employees, customers, business, and bank accounts by implementing everything they learn as it pertains to employee and customer safety, health, and security. They will be safer because of it and so will your loved ones. Make no mistake about it - the scrutiny will be harsh for everyone involved. The decision makers will be picked at and scrutinized thoroughly, but so will the employees and the vendors.

And I, for one, am tired of seeing restaurants fail. That's because...

Restaurants Move Us

It's true! ... Many of the most important things that happen in our lives are celebrated in restaurants, and in conjunction with a meal – birthdays, first dates, anniversaries, reunions, and celebrations – to name just a few.

In fact, there is no better way – even in this high-tech, internet-driven world that we all live in – to bond relationships, celebrate milestones, learn life's lessons or enjoy idle chit-chat with a dear friend than to sit down at a table and break bread. Restaurants are among the world's first social networks and the place where real life emotional experiences play out for us all.

These are the precious moments that determine who we are and what we truly value; because, in restaurants, people actually sit across from one another and engage by sharing thoughts, dreams, and secrets.

But, during these challenging times, we cannot ignore the enormous economic impact that restaurants play in our lives, as well. America relies on restaurants for daily sustenance;

and, without restaurants of varying types, we would have neither convenient nor affordable access to the much-needed meals that allow us as a society to move forward in our ongoing efforts to strive and thrive. And, according to research, 92-percent of Americans say they enjoy going to restaurants – confirming that dining in a restaurant is one of America's favorite pastimes that impacts nearly every man, woman, and child in the country. But that still doesn't tell the whole story ...

Restaurants are the second largest employment workforce in the country – employing between 11 and 12 percent of the entire U.S. workforce; and the restaurant industry is supported by more than 150,000 product and service providers that employ millions more.

The numbers become truly staggering when one realizes that more than 50 percent of the population has worked in a restaurant at some point in their lifetime.

Furthermore, 9 out of 10 restaurants nationwide participate in charitable activities that help to support the local communities that they do business in; and, each year, restaurants provide an estimated $3 billion in charitable contributions.

Make no mistake about it, restaurants are an American institution like no other and impact us all – in ways that no other industry can.

Whether it is fast food or fine dining, casual or convenient, a bit extravagant or downright downhome, what we eat and the restaurants where we choose to share these meal occasions are deeply personal – after all, not only are we putting the food and drink created by restaurants and restaurant employees into our bodies, but we are creating special moments with those we care most about that will often be a part of our memories for years, and even decades, to come.

Take a few moments to reminisce about the grandest achievements and fondest memories of your life, and I am quite certain that you will realize that many of them took place in restaurants.

Perhaps it was the local diner where you stole your first kiss, or maybe it was the fine dining establishment where "Mr. Right" popped the question … or maybe the pizza place where your son wildly celebrated his birthday or the coffee shop where you enjoyed the last long chat with the uncle who taught you how to fish. Maybe you will recall the fast-food place with the perfect French fries, or the little bistro where you asked your best friend to be your maid of honor. Maybe you will remember the steak house where you got your first job, or the franchised restaurant where you were given the opportunity to build a career so you could buy your first home …

These are the real moments that truly make a lasting impact on our lives and the lives of those nearest and dearest to our hearts, and it is in these restaurants where we laugh and smile, listen and cry, love and live, work and grow.

Restaurants are spread throughout the world, but no society

on the face of the earth relies on restaurants the way America does. And nowhere can one find the choices, diversity, excellence, and convenience provided by restaurants here within these United States and, just like American families, restaurants come in all shapes, styles, and sizes – with each and every one of them playing a critically important role in the overall picture.

We can rely on and experience a wide range of service styles from fine dining to quick casual, and from casual dining to fast food and everything in between. We can savor the absolute best cuisines from French to Italian, from Japanese to Greek, from Chinese to Indian, and from American to Mexican.

We can savor the best flavor profiles, the best burgers and fries, the best pizzas and pastas, the best chicken, steak, seafood and pork entrees, and the absolute widest varieties of appetizers, salads, desserts, and beverages.

America offers the fastest, the most convenient, the most affordable, and the most outstanding restaurants in the world.

If you think I love restaurants… you are absolutely right!

In fact, as a society, Americans have had a long-standing love affair with restaurants that has lasted for many, many years and now with the high visibility of celebrity chefs, cooking contests, restaurant reviews, and restaurant TV shows and Food networks... restaurants are more popular than ever.

I, personally, began to gain my passion for restaurants on a memorable Friday night in 1978. That's when I got my first real job working in the dish pit of a local steakhouse in Boaz, Wisconsin.

I'll never forget that first intense experience – the feeling of shock when the waitresses handed me crinkled-up dollar bills and handfuls of change from their aprons, the memory of savoring my first-ever New York Strip steak with potatoes and corn, the confidence gained when I was handed my first paycheck, and how proud I was of myself when I received a promotion from busboy to waiter.

My childhood was tough, and I cannot express in words how badly a nearly blind, scrawny, fatherless, basically friendless, 14-year-old boy needed something – anything – to hang his hat on.

Quite frankly, I look back now, and I know for certain it was this love of restaurants, and all that they are, that challenged me, drove me, provided for me ... and saved me by the Grace of God.

Many years have passed for me since that first night, and I cherish every milestone achieved and feel a deep sense of pride, accomplishment, and belonging because of each of them.

It is with this continued passion for restaurants – an industry that has provided for me, my family, my people, and my customers – along with the endless array of memories seared deep in my soul, and the ever-growing number of opportunities still out in front of us all, that inspires me to ask you to help me in my mission to bring awareness of the severe and life altering damages caused by slip and falls in America's restaurants from coast to coast and the strategies that can help reduce these preventable tragedies.

That is my main motivation behind writing this book, to increase awareness of these restaurant specific risks and help those navigating these waters when the time comes.

All glory goes to God for the opportunities, the blessings, and the gifts. Thank you, Lord.

EPILOGUE
Who to Call When Restaurants Go Wrong

O F COURSE, IF you require our services, we are here, and just a mere phone call away.

When a restaurant customer, owner, manager, insurer, or personal injury attorney finds themselves involved in a lawsuit or insurance claim or investigated in the pitfall of one of these terrible tragedies, the entire process and events will be dissected in ways no one ever before imagined was possible.

In full disclosure, that dissection is what I do for a living.

In fact, a forensic expert's job is to go back and try to dig through every little detail, fact, and piece of evidence, to determine what happened, why it happened, what was done right and

wrong, and who is responsible for anything and everything that took place.

I will be looking for anything out of compliance and outside of what is described as the reasonable and customary industry standards that took place before, during, and even after the subject incident.

No case I opine on can be filed away as run-of-the-mill, or not all that important, or not that big of deal when a person is getting injured, harmed, sickened, maimed, or killed. Ever. Every case I have ever dealt with has a significant impact on the people involved and those that love and care for them.

If you need to know more about me or what I do, feel free to Google me or Wikipedia me (Howard Cannon) or my company (Restaurant Expert Witness) or conduct whatever other resaerch you think is important and necessary.

For now, I can tell you that I am a court-testifying Forensic Scientist and Expert Witness with more than 300 litigation and 350 pre-litigation/consulting cases to my credit in state and federal courts across the United States and in markets around the globe.

I have authored several books including 'The Complete Idiot's Guide to Starting Your Own Restaurant' © (2001), 'The Complete Idiot's Guide to Starting a Restaurant - Second Edition' © (2005), and 'Restaurant OSHA Safety and Security:

The Book of Restaurant Industry Standards and Best Practices'
© (2016).

In 1978 as a teenager, I started my restaurant industry career washing dishes and have since held nearly every conceivable restaurant industry position from busboy to President and from barback to Chief Operating Officer.

In 1987, I launched Restaurant Operations Institute, the parent company for Restaurant Expert Witness and my writing, research, and training business.

Lawyers, judges, and juries rely on my unbiased expertise and professional opinions in a wide variety of cases impacting the restaurant and bar industries across America and around the globe.

For more information about Restaurant Expert Witness, Restaurant Operations Institute, and/or myself visit RestaurantExpertWitness.com, visit the associated social sites, go to Wikipedia, Amazon, Google, or YouTube, email us at porter@RestaurantExpertWitness.com, or call our corporate office at 800.300.5764.

Kindest regards and God's richest blessings to you going forward.

Works Cited

Our research for this book consisted of the following – some of which has been cited in the text:

United States v. Carroll Towing; Learned Hand; About OSHA Page; HACCP Principles & Application Guidelines _ FDA Hazard Analysis...; Hazard Analysis ritical Control Point (HACCP) 2022; FDA, Managing Food Safety, HACCP (cover +); HACCP - First Principle - Identify and Analyze (sic) Hazards; Emergency Preparedness and Response_ Getting Started _ Occupational Safety...; Guidance on Preparing Workplaces for an Influenza Pandemic; Guide to Restaurant Safety; Centers for Disease Control and Prevention; OSHA-At-A-Glance; OSHA's General Duty Clause; OSHA Law & Regulations; Directorate of Cooperative and State Programs _ State Plans; OSHA 1926 Subpart C; Safety and Health Management Systems; Safety training and education. _ Occupational Safety and Health...; eCFR __ 29 CFR 1910.9 -- Compliance duties owed to each employee; Food Service Sanitation Environment; OSHA Job Safety and Health_ It's the Law! (Wall Poster); Compliance Assistance Quick Start - General Industry _ Occupational Safety...; Subpart C Safety and Health Program Management; osha2254; Emergency action plans. - 1910.38; About OSHA _ Occupational Safety and Health Administration; Safety Systems and Sub-Systems; Years of OSHA Enforcement; OSHA Cites Republic Engineered Products; Memorandum from Bruce Hillenbrand; OSHA Issues New Directive to Keep Communication Tower Workers Safe; OSHA Orders Safety Upgrades after 7-ton Buoy; Cabinet Manufacturer Oak Creations; Excavation and Trenching are among the Most Hazardous; OSHA Workers' Rights; OSHA 1926 Subpart C; Safety and Health Management Systems; OSHA Safety Plans Library - Written Safety Plan; Compliance Assistance Quick Start - General Industry _ Occupational Safety...; hazardcommunication; OSHA Standards Protection on the Job; OSHA1507; Compliance Assistance Quick Start - General Industry _ Occupational Safety...; 1910.38 - Emergency action plans. _ Occupational Safety and Health...; eTools _ Evacuation Plans and Procedures eTool - Do I Need an Emergency...; osha2254; OSHA - Employer Responsibilities; Definitions applicable to this subpart. - 1910.399; osha3170; STD 01-01-012 - STD 1-1.12 - Application of 29 CFR 1910.27, Fixed Ladders; Shipyard Employment eTool; Construction eTool _ Falls - Ladder Safety; Guide for Protecting Workers from Woodworking Hazards; Definitions applicable to this subpart. - 1910.399; OSHA Law & Regulations; OSHA Safety Manual Software Template; Job Hazard Analysis; Personal Protective Equipment; Lumley Insurance; PLRMG800_Cafe and Restaurant Risk Management...; American National - Identifying Liability Hazards in Restaurants; Restaurant & Food Services; Property & Liability; Slips and Falls Study; Compliance Assistance Quick Start - General Industry _ Occupational Safety...; Restaurant & Food Services; Walking & Working Surfaces Checklist; Nelson & Associates __ Premises __ Five Types of Same-Level Falls; Slip, Trips & Falls-Identification & Prevention

This isn't a court case, so there might be more. Just go to OHSA.gov, HACAP, ADA, FDA, and if you still have a question, feel free to do your own research or just contact us.

www.ingramcontent.com/pod-product-compliance
Lightning Source LLC
Chambersburg PA
CBHW011159220326
41597CB00026BA/4672